RISE AN

The Condomini

Hans Ibelings a
Edited by Nicola Spunt

The Architecture Observer

CONTENTS

PREFACE
Alexander Josephson

This all began in 2014 at two not-so-fluke parties. The first was at Art Metropole, Toronto's premier venue for multi-media artist publications. I was there to attend a book launch that one of my favourite architecture critics, Hans Ibelings, was hosting for a recent graduate of University of Toronto's Daniels Faculty of Architecture, Landscape, and Design. He and I had both recently started lecturing at U of T, but I hadn't yet had a chance to meet him. I planted myself by the bar knowing it was just a matter of time before the tall Dutch academic would eventually need a drink.

The second party was a huge debate at The Theater Center on Queen Street West where I was invited to speak on a panel that deliberated the question of whether the City of Toronto needed to install a new position: a municipal Creative Director. The moderator was an intrepid intellectual named Nicola Spunt, a doctor of English Literature and founder of After School, the speaker series that organized the talk.

These events sparked the beginning of friendships that turned into bona fide collaborations, with Nicola eventually becoming Director of Content & Culture at PARTISANS and Hans a frequent guest at our studio. This book is the outcome of our shared interest in and love for Toronto.

At its core PARTISANS represents the idea that architecture is a political act and has the power to mould larger social values and experiences. Architecture is more than building buildings; it has political and cultural ramifications and represents our civilization's collective will to realize its necessities as well as its fantasies.

Rise and Sprawl is the second installation of PARTISANS' research into the city we call home. The first stab was a satirical critique of Toronto in the wake of former Mayor Rob Ford's five-year tenure: *Suburbylonia: Will This Boom Be Toronto's Doom?* The graphic novel pokes at the establishment in a light-hearted way and takes all parties to task for Toronto's middle-of-the-road approach to architecture and planning in the face of great economic and social prosperity. We were just starting out at the time; nobody was really hiring us yet. *Suburbylonia* was our attempt to hack our way into having a voice about the shape and future of development in the city.

In the process of researching and searching for a way to tell a relevant story about our city, we began to realize that one of the most unique things happening to Toronto was its intensification in the form of a phenomenon we have called "condominiumization." The PARTISANS team began a formal, bottom-up architectural inquiry into the phenomenon using the data sets that have turned Toronto into a bit of an urban *cause célèbre* and earned it international rankings as one of the greatest places to live in the world. What follows are the results of years' long efforts to describe Toronto's condominiumization as well as a catalogue that anatomizes the condominium in a bid to contextualize this unprecedented era of urbanization.

The first section is an essay by Hans describing the advent of the condominium in the architectural development of Toronto. It is a historical framing and critical analysis of the emergence of what could be described as a flash-fried vernacular.

The second section is a catalogue by PARTISANS that deconstructs the condominium forms and typologies that are being built en masse in Toronto.

The third section is an animated call to action for how we can make our city—and maybe even the world—a better place through better architecture. It also strives to dissect the process by which architecture is approved in the city and proposes some alternatives for how to practice, plan, and build differently to maximize everyone's best interests.

Rise and Sprawl aims to open up a conversation. As we like to say at PARTISANS, join us.

Hans Ibelings and PARTISANS

RISE AND SPRAWL

INTRODUCTION

TOWER BY TOWER

Hans Ibelings

1.
This is not the first time this expression has been used. Robert Galston, Research Assistant at the Institute of Urban Studies at the University of Winnipeg, runs a blog under the name "The Rise and Sprawl" (http://riseandsprawl. blogspot.ca), which was only discovered after work began on this publication.

2.
Preville, Philip. "The Divided City: Toronto's Gilded Age Never Made It To The Suburbs." *Toronto Life*, 13 February 2014. Web.

This is the story of Toronto's condo towers, and how the city has become what it is today.

The rise and sprawl of the condo tower is undeniably the city's most remarkable development in recent years. The number of towers, their size, mass, volume, height, and the speed by which they are built is astounding.[1] The only thing that isn't remarkable about the rise and sprawl of Toronto's condo towers is their architecture.

Comparable condo booms have occurred and are unfolding in other cities as well, but what sets Toronto apart is the scale of its transformation, especially in its urban core. Until the late 1990s, Toronto was a predominantly horizontal city, with some office towers downtown and a few clusters of 1960s residential high-rises situated in green expanses scattered throughout the urban landscape. This horizontal city still exists, but has been overlaid by a vertical one that mainly consists of ever-higher residential towers.

Since the turn of the twenty-first century, approximately 80,000 condo units have been built in Toronto or are currently under construction; a comparable number is in the planning pipeline. This brings the total number up to nearly 250,000 new condo units since 2000. Between 2006 and 2014, downtown's population increased by 18 per cent.[2]

Hence, Toronto is experiencing a double movement of people coming into the city and towers going up into the air. And now that so much of the low-hanging fruit of easily developable downtown land—yesteryear's parking lots—has been snapped up, towers are starting to sprawl out and spring up in increasingly less central locations.

One doesn't have to be an architectural connoisseur to see that Toronto's condo boom hasn't produced much, if any, outstanding architecture. This offers an intriguing paradox. The rise and sprawl of condo towers has led to enormous wealth creation and made Toronto a much more lively city. It has also given the city a sky-line, and a pretty impressive one for that matter. But it hasn't yielded architectural treasures. A large majority of the condo architecture is bland, interchangeable, and forgettable. Moreover, details are often crude, finishings shabby, and floor plans crammed. This is not to suggest that there are no talented architects involved, but the bottom line seems to be that developers' interests trump design excellence.

And yet, even though most new condo buildings are, artistically considered, disappointing, and the final project is rarely better than the first design, they are fascinating as a cultural phenomenon, as architecture minus the art of architecture. Part of the fascination, at least for an architectural historian, is that they offer a rare opportunity to witness the emergence and propagation of a tradition, and the swift development of a new, pressure-cooked vernacular, based on a limited set of building typologies, materials, forms, and colour schemes. Vernaculars normally evolve over long periods of time as knowledge, skills, conventions, and habits are passed on from one generation to the next. In defiance of this normal trajectory, the vernacular of Toronto's high-rise condos has been churned out within the span of a single generation.

The condo tower vernacular is exceptional not only because of the speed with which is has surfaced, but also because of the conditions of its emergence. Whereas vernacular architecture is typically built by users themselves, here it has been wrought by a condo-industrial complex. The word 'vernacular' is usually shorthand for architecture without architects. In the case of Toronto's towers it is the opposite: it is architects without architecture.

Financial Tool
Even when accomplished designers like Frank Gehry, Daniel Libeskind, and Moshe Safdie (for whom developers

3.
Hanes, Tracy.
"Condo Act Revolu-
tionized Housing
Market in Ontario."
Toronto Star,
23 February 2008. Web.

usually reserve epithets like "world class" or "celebrity") propose new buildings for Toronto, it seems they have no choice but to dilute their visions. If one compares the initial and subsequent designs for two recently proposed high-rise projects by Gehry and Safdie, respectively, it is obvious that even if the buildings themselves do not get downsized, their architectural ambitions certainly do. This diminishment seems an invariable effect of form following finance: if the return on investment has to go up, the level of architecture needs to come down. Return on investment is a self-evident credo of the condo-industrial complex, which is a money multiplier by design. Alvin Rosenberg, who among many other things was the author of *Condominium in Canada* and the founding president of the Canadian Condominium Institute, acknowledged as much in a 2008 interview with the Toronto Star. He noted that "one of the big advantages" of the Condominium Act was that it allowed for shared ownership, which enabled developers "to make more money by selling the units individually as private homes, rather than selling the project as a whole."[3] Rosenberg's comments underline the fact that the condo tower isn't primarily an architectural construction or a tool for building cities, but first and foremost a financial instrument. Its architectural quality is what graphic design is to a bank note: it adds nothing to its monetary value. This lack of emphasis on the architecture itself is corroborated by marketing slogans that advertise new condo projects, but rarely ever mention the word 'architecture,' let alone name the architect.

So far the condo market has generated lucrative business opportunities for developers and investors, even during the recent housing market crisis, which more or less bypassed Canada and certainly Toronto. Given developers' and investors' understandable wish to make a profit, the aim is to optimize the balance between land value, construction costs, and revenue. This drives

up the building height, and due to the small size of most plots, the high-rise usually becomes a tower. *Quod erat demonstrandum* why Toronto has so many condo towers.

With little regulation in place—it is telling that one of the most important city documents on the subject, the Tall Building Design Guidelines, is a set of non-legally binding recommendations—it comes down to the negotiating skills of the developers. Their goal is to see how high they can go and how far they can stretch and bend the rules, often leveraging their cause with the City and the Ontario Municipal Board (OMB) by arguing that other buildings in the vicinity have already bypassed zoning rules in a similar way.

Ur-condo

As with many vernaculars, the Toronto condo tower's origin isn't totally clear. Of course there was no condo tower before there was a high-rise or the Condominium Act, which made 'condominium,' aka 'strata title,' a legal term.[4] One building is often considered Canada's first high-rise condominium, but it is not in Toronto; it is in Ottawa: Horizon House. This project was started in 1969 and completed one year later. The developer, Minto, is a familiar name in Toronto.[5] Horizon House, the very first high-rise with strata titles, doesn't look like any recent condo project, though. It looks much more like contemporary public housing complexes, which were usually massive slabs or stubby towers, and not like the slender tower of today. So even if Horizon House is in theory the ur-condo, it is only so in genotype and not in its phenotypic presentation, which bears little resemblance to the characteristic sleekness of its successors.

The history of condo towers in Canada also owes a debt to China. It is commonly acknowledged that the condo towers of Toronto took cues from its long-distance relative, Vancouver, whose 1990s residential

4.
"Condominiums have existed since time immemorial. In fact, the concept of a condominium has accompanied many urban civilizations, with a sophisticated legal code existing in Roman law." Mullin, Robert M. "Condominium Disputes & A.D.R.: A Recipe for Confusion?" Web.

5.
Langston, Patrick. "Minto Communities Marks 60th Anniversary." *Ottawa Citizen*, 5 June 2015. Web.

6.
Pigg, Susan. "Investors Own Less Than a Quarter of Toronto Condominiums: CMHC Annual Housing Report Takes Revealing Look at Canada's Exploding Condo Sector." *Toronto Star*, 18 December 2013. Web; Pigg, Susan. "Percentage of Toronto Condos Owned By Foreign Investors Is Very Low, CMHC Says." *Toronto Star*, 16 December 2014; "Toronto's 'Condo King' Says 50% of Condos Are Foreign-Owned." CBC News, 12 August 2014, Web; Gray, John. "Foreign Buyers Own 10 Per Cent of Toronto's Newest Condos: CMHC." *BNN*, April 7, 2016. Web.

high-rises are allegedly descended from China, having migrated from Hong Kong alongside the influx of Chinese newcomers to Canada. The link between the Chinese and condo towers is a persistent one. Although hard data is difficult to source, anecdotal evidence suggests there is a high level of Chinese investment in Vancouver's condo market.

While the vast majority of the new residential high-rise buildings are legally speaking condominiums, many of the strata are inhabited by tenants, not unit owners, blurring the difference between a condo and a rental apartment. It is estimated that somewhere between 23 and 40 per cent of the total number of Toronto's condo units (again, hard data is hard to come by) is privately owned as an investment and rented out. Non-Canadians make up a portion of these investors, but figures for international ownership vary greatly: some say 2.4 per cent, others cite 1 in 10 in the downtown core, while other statistics suggest that anywhere between 17 per cent or 'about half' of all condos are owned by foreigners. Toronto has earned a reputation as a safe place to park one's money. It became attractive in the aftermath of the 2008 global financial crisis, which Canada weathered relatively well, and it is now going through another wave of popularity as the alarming slowdown of economic growth in China since 2014 is leading to a flight of capital from that country.[6]

No matter what the exact percentage of foreign investment is, it has probably contributed to the ongoing rise of property prices, which is outpacing the average increase in salaries by a lot. There is obviously more to this story, but if prices are rising faster than income, the market is verging into the territory of what is commonly defined as a housing bubble. This bubble makes it harder for starters to join the party. For them, owning a condo, or, more precisely, obtaining a mortgage for a condo, is becoming increasingly difficult. One visible effect is that

developers have started to offer one-bedroom-plus-den units, which, despite their small size, boast two bathrooms. Even more economical versions feature one bathroom with two doors. This enables owners on a tight budget to rent out the den, skirting the building code requirement that a bedroom must have a window, and offers the second tenant, at the very least, the privacy of one's own bathroom door.

Ever-rising prices are spurring an increased demand for rental units, as many just simply can't afford to buy into the market. Not only is this triggering more people and companies to invest in condos as rental properties, it is also slowly leading to the development of rental apartment projects. Thus far, this isn't having any effect on building design. As is the case with condo architecture, everything is driven by different short- and long-term financial constructions. From a critic's perspective, even when these buildings are or become rental apartment towers, they still look like condo towers, with the same characteristics that make them so fascinating.

Logic
Odd as it may sound, a huge part of the strange appeal of the new condo towers is that they all look more or less the same. This is obviously one of the essences of a vernacular. In many rural regions, for example, farmhouses resemble one another; they're all comprised of similar shapes, materials, colours, and details, and deploy the same construction methods. Although the Toronto condo vernacular is still very young (and it remains to be seen if it will ever get a chance to age), it is immediately recognizable as well. Yet, the two cornerstones that typically drive a vernacular—context and climate—don't seem to have factored into the rise of Toronto's condos. It could be maintained that the presence of quarries and cement factories in the city's vicinity offer an explanation for the prevalence of

concrete constructions. But beyond that, there is hardly any specificity to the generic glass and metal cladding, and it goes without saying that the materials and methods of building do not respond to Toronto's extreme climate, which sees temperatures fluctuate between minus 25 and plus 35 degrees Celsius. This makes the current condo tower a strangely decontextualized and climactically dissonant vernacular. It obeys it own self-contained axiom, all the while deploying the ingredients that formed the foundation of modern architecture—glass, steel, and concrete—yet without pursuing any of the ideals of modernism or mirroring its attempts at innovating architecture.

Market logic is one important explanation for this sameness. As long as condos sell there is no incentive to change anything, and as long as there is nothing else on the market, people will buy what's available. It is possible that people are soothed by the justification that, as long as they buy a condo that is comparable to all other condos, it will eventually be easy to sell it again. This logic of the housing market is a bit like the Abilene Paradox, which suggests that all parties involved are making decisions based on what they believe others would prefer, and hence nobody ends up with an outcome they actually like.

What makes this even more of a riveting paradox is the extent to which the actual living spaces tend to defy practicality and common sense. As if there hasn't been a glorious century of magnificent innovations in housing design. As if the whole idea of combining efficiency with comfort, which forms the basis of "Wohnung für das Existenzminimum," was never invented. Looking at all of these almost identical, almost always substandard condo floor plans, one can draw the conclusion that dwellers settle for less, both in size and quality. It leaves one to wonder about the power of condo marketing. Is the aspirational lifestyle promise so seductive as to lull con-sumers into overlooking all the material insufficiencies?

It is still too early to fully grasp all the layers of obscured meaning that shore up the phenomenon of condominium culture. Hopefully with some distance and a bit of hindsight, historians and anthropologists of the future will be able to distill the deepest longings of the *homo condomini* in early twenty-first century Toronto. What does the open concept convey about the sense of home or about human relations? What does the often substantially sized kitchen in those tiny studios reveal about the symbolic importance of gastronomic rituals in an age when people are spending less and less time cooking? What is the practical purpose of the tiny den, which is often included in even the smallest of condos? What is the deeper significance of this dark, windowless space, which hints at a multitude of potentials (man cave, family room, library, home theatre) if only it were bigger than a closet? What is the symbolic meaning of the number ten given that many condos boast to ten-foot ceilings in at least part of the unit?

All of these questions arise because it is hard to see the functional and aesthetic rationales for many of the decisions that inform condo design. When one reviews the layouts of several buildings, it appears that most kitchens, for example, are the same throughout an entire building, independent of the size of the unit. This kind of design decision is likely fuelled by efficiency and economy, even though it ultimately doesn't make proportional sense. By the same logic, it would seem that the main advantage of an open-concept design is that it allows for the construction of even smaller units. Minimizing the need for walls and doors is another way to save on building costs. That the windowless den is accepted as an apparently inevitable by-product of a not-so-great floor plan is also confounding. The significance of the ten-foot ceiling undoubtedly has something to do with the attraction of round numbers and Canadians' incomplete transition to the metric

7.
Living in Downtown and the Centres. Toronto: City of Toronto, 2012: 5. Web.

system. And the commonly featured floor-to-ceiling windows are likely the cheapest to install and most effective way of directing the dwellers' view outward to the cityscape and away from the unit's invariable design flaws. Sometimes this view actually reveals Toronto's heady skyline. But most of the time it offers a mirror image: a reflection off a neighbouring condo.

Penthouse

It is a commonplace oversimplification to speak of the purported opposition between Toronto's entitled downtown elite in their fancy condos and the hardworking taxpayers in the suburbs. This polarization was a favourite trope of the late mayor Rob Ford. Contrary to generally held ideas that downtown Toronto is the territory of the high-earning, happy few, which would seem to be corroborated by rapidly rising property prices, the truth is that income distribution within the downtown doesn't differ that much from the Greater Toronto Area as a whole. (The exception is that the highest income bracket remains overrepresented in the city centre.) Downtown Toronto has significant outliers at the low end, with more than 20 per cent of household incomes below $20,000 per year. The latter is most likely due to the presence of large numbers of students. At the high end, almost 20 per cent of downtown households earn incomes above $150,000 per year.[7] Some of the high earners living downtown inhabit condominiums, but since the average detached house is much more expensive than the average condo, the overlap between condos and high earners is probably limited. In other words, a large majority of condo dweller sits somewhere in this nebulous field called the middle class.

Zeroing in on condo buildings, one finds substantial differences between the haves and have-nots. The have-nots lack space and views. Many small units are tucked away on the lower levels, sometimes simultaneously facing the backs of other buildings,

alleys, and northward. There is a whole other universe for those who have it all—ample space and generous views at the top, although the top units rarely stand out in an architectural sense. Traditionally, the classic penthouse was the crown of a skyscraper. In this era of condominiumization, designating a setback for a penthouse would waste too many sellable square meters. Hence, instead of one penthouse, most towers feature multiple penthouse units, often spread out over several higher-level floors. Just as the have-nots share their dusky fate somewhere down below, those living in the rarified upper strata share a diluted signifier of privilege. What used to be a unique unit that bested all others has become the generic name for many units near the top. If the semiotic and spatial signification of the penthouse continues, it will only be a matter of time before the arrival of the all-penthouse tower (which will almost certainly be called The Penthouse).

Collectivism
The democratization of the penthouse is evidence of a pattern: despite being the product of undisguised capitalism, the contemporary condo bears more than a hint of communism, especially if one considers how many collective facilities are included. The dream of collective housing born out of revolutionary Russia and attempted in projects like Moscow's Narkomfin Building has been revamped for a capitalist context. Narkomfin's architect, Moisei Ginzburg, promoted his architecture as a social condenser. And while he himself never managed to carry out more than a single magnificent project, his program has become a reality nearly a century later. The hedonistic setting of Toronto's condo towers is grounded in a form of collectivism, with shared amenities such as pools, spas, gyms, yoga studios, roof terraces, party rooms, lounge-like lobbies, and libraries. Just as Narkomfin's dream of collectivity remained largely unfulfilled—it turned out not everybody

liked sharing a kitchen—not all communal facilities in every condo tower are equally successful either. This is likely due to their atmosphere and overall appearance, which is often less impressive than the seductive pre-construction renderings used to bait prospective buyers.

Those deceptive renderings almost always portray healthy, wealthy, good-looking people having a great time in what resembles the lobby of a boutique hotel or enjoying a summer evening on a rooftop patio (if units are shown at all, they are usually empty, denuded of human inhabitants).

In this context, it is also important to consider the language that accompanies the marketing imagery, which rarely mentions anything about the actual architecture. The location—often an 'iconic address'—has more value than the architecture of the building itself. That the architecture isn't marketed as a unique selling point of condos bespeaks a classic chicken-and-egg situation. Because the architecture is often mediocre, it has no marketing value. And because it is possible to sell condos without great architecture, there appears to be no point in investing in design quality.

The condo tower and its architecture are usually treated as separate entities. The tower follows the unwritten rules of condominium vernacular, whereas the architecture is at most an extra, generally subordinated to the branding. Although the branding is sometimes high-end, as in the case of Art Shoppe's collaboration with Karl Lagerfeld, most of the time it is trite and hackneyed. But no matter how shallow, marketing is still more important than the architectural design. So a hierarchy emerges: first comes the spreadsheet, which subsequently determines the building structure, and then comes the packaging and the advertising. The architectural exercise that happens in between almost becomes irrelevant. Put another way, the condo tower isn't driven by architectural considerations.

Talented architects may in fact be working on a project, but their creative contribution is not only secondary to finances and marketing, it has become expendable.

Just as the condo tower has become unmoored from its architecture, there is a similar disconnect between most towers and their surrounding urban landscape. To a large extent, they are indifferent to their context, even if occasionally some version of heritage or nostalgic window-dressing is used to evoke the site's history by retaining an historical name or saving bits and pieces and pieces of older, original buildings and integrating them into new towers. This form of preservation, if it deserves that name, creates a Potemkin version of a past Toronto, unconvincingly suggesting that the new city hasn't entirely wiped out the old one.

The architectural past, which is allegedly maintained through these acts of façadism, rarely inspires the new design. Moreover, these attempts at so-called preservation are, for the most part, not especially elegant or well integrated; they're just there, with the new architecture completely indifferent to whatever the past may have been. This is the essence of many condo towers: their relationship to context has everything to do with filling a plot of land with as much volume as possible. In fact, if it would fit the footprint of another site, the condo tower could equally sprout there. And no one would likely even notice. In the best cases, there is a podium at the bottom of the tower that makes a more or less successful attempt to become somewhat accessible to the public, but usually condo towers are introverted stand-alones, contributing nothing in particular to the city, other than being dispensable.

Suburban Values
With respect to indifference to context, Toronto's condo towers obey a similar logic to the housing developments

8.
Warzecha, Monika.
"The suite life:
A timeline of the
condo's early
history in Canada."
Buzzbuzzhome,
26 February 2014.
Web.

that populate the suburbs. If suburbia has become more or less synonymous with the 'cookie-cutter,' then the same homogenizing kitchen tool could be invoked to describe the effects of condominiumization on Toronto. As incongruous as it might seem, the condo tower in fact owes more to the suburbs than it does the city. Like most binaries, the distinction between city and suburb is often a questionable one, as it obscures some fundamental relationships between the two regions. In many ways, the suburbs are just a continuation of the city, and while it is hard to substantiate with more than anecdotal evidence, the condo tower seems to have brought suburbia to town. Many condo dwellers have a suburban background, which isn't surprising in a heavily suburban country like Canada. Yet, what is potentially surprising is the fact that many of these new urban dwellers haven't been assimilated by the city and its ways. Instead, condominiums seem to play a role in making it possible for former suburbanites to retain the values and live out the ideals characteristic of suburban living. Condos offer a relatively hassle-free, detached way of life, much like the newer homes in the suburbs. The rise of big-box stores in downtown Toronto, which often occupy the base of condo buildings, are ideal for buying groceries once a week, and the arrival of traditionally suburban restaurant chains are further evidence that the condo tower has become a vehicle for the suburbanization of the city core. In the same vein, the suburban backyard has been relocated to the condo tower rooftop in the form of a sky yard.

The idea that the condo is the urban version of a house in the suburbs has a bit of a history in Canada. In "The suite life: A timeline of the condo's early history in Canada," Monika Warzecha cites a 1970 publication that promoted a condo project as offering "suburban-type living in downtown Edmonton."[8] To a certain extent, the same idea undergirds Moshe Safdie's Habitat 67 in

Montreal. Habitat 67 was an experiment in stacking the proverbial suburban house with a garden one on top of the other (which is to say nothing of the fact that the building was erected in a part of town that has never been particularly urban to begin with). Edmonton and Montreal half a century ago were different places than they are today, and certainly they aren't Toronto. But self-consciously or not, condos right across Canada riff on the suburban lifestyle. The latter has always been symbolized by the detached house, and while condos are by definition units within a multi-unit building, they nevertheless purvey the same kind of detachedness many dream of finding in the suburbs. Sure, one has neighbours and shared access to collective spaces, like party rooms and lobbies, but condos are not communal living spaces. They cater to people who are generally happy to go home and close out the rest of the world. The rare moments of conviviality around the occasional shared summer barbecue on a rooftop terrace are generally the exception that underlines the rule. The only thing condo dwellers definitely share is a condo fee.

9.
Aira, César.
Varamo. New York:
New Horizon, 2012:
89. Print.

Pre-and Protohistory

Condo towers are a relatively new phenomenon in Toronto, but as the Argentinian novelist César Aira has remarked, "novelty makes its causes new, giving birth to them retrospectively."[9] The condo towers are at once a break with the city's past and at the same time a product of that very past. Toronto's current condo boom is shaped by a pre-and protohistory. The prehistory corresponds to the early period after the Second World War when Toronto was starting to become a modern city. Large, freestanding residential towers and slabs in the suburbs started to go up. Some of these slabs emerged in even more central locations, like St. James Town, the usual Toronto scape-goat for all the wrongs of modernist planning.

10.
Anthony Flint,
author of the book
*Wrestling with Moses:
How Jane Jacobs
Took On New York's
Master Builder
and Transformed the
American City* is
quoted in: Garner,
Dwight. "When David
Fought Goliath in
Washington Square
Park." *The New York
Times*, 4 August 2009.
Web.

In accordance with the functionalism of the era, these suburban residential areas were spatially separated from places of work in the downtown area. The latter were becoming, in the parlance of the day, a CBD (Central Business District), which only thrived during office hours. The suburbs and the CBD were conveniently connected by urban highways, such as the Gardiner Expressway and Allen Road, although public opposition cut the latter short of becoming the north-south Spadina Expressway. The decision not to extend the Allen was one of the symbolic moments that not only marked a Pyrrhic victory for those who wished to curb car traffic in the city, but also the end of the slab residential high-rise's reign and the beginning of an era during which this type of modernization started to be vilified.

The patron saint of opposition to modernization and modern planning was mixed-use and sidewalk advocate Jane Jacobs. Jacobs came to Toronto in 1968, bringing with her the fame she earned for the highly successful, and highly overrated, *The Death and Life of Great American Cities*, whose greatest achievement is its single-mindedness. One gets a full picture of the book's message just by reading the table of contents: professional planners got it wrong, everybody else knows better. Despite the ostensible straightforwardness of her pedestrian urbanism, which takes aim at modern architecture and planning, it wasn't modernism but Big Government she considered to be the real problem. Jacobs moved to Toronto from New York where she had rallied against everything the prodigious planner Robert Moses stood for and had accomplished. Moses's legacy, in the words of his biographer Anthony Flint, encompassed "13 bridges, 2 tunnels, 637 miles of highways, 658 playgrounds, 10 giant public swimming pools, 17 state parks plus a large number of new or renovated city parks," not to mention a large number of housing projects.[10] For Jacobs, Moses represented

the kind of top-down planning she scorned. It is possible that her deep dislike of Big Government may have developed during her tenure as editor of the Cold War propaganda magazine, *Amerika Illustrated*, whose target audience were citizens of the USSR, the country that epitomized Big Government more than any other at the time.[11]

Jacobs' aversion to top-down anything is usually interpreted as a bottom-up-small-is-beautiful ethos; however, upon closer consideration, she seems to have been more of an adherent to the *laissez-faire* school, almost as zealous as Russian-born American Ayn Rand in her belief that the alleged invisible hand of the market would do its beneficial work in the city as well as everywhere else.[12] Richard Florida, another American city sage who moved to Toronto, recalls one of their conversations in a piece for *The Atlantic*: "I asked her specifically about her views toward gentrification…. She pointed to the difference between the heavy hand of government-sponsored urban renewal programs and the complex workings of urban real estate markets. She went on to describe how cities have an amazing capacity to reorganize and reenergize themselves. The dulling down of one neighbourhood, as the diversity of social and economic life was sucked out of it, would lead invariably to the rise of new, energized neighbourhoods elsewhere in the city. And then in what remains my single favourite comment of hers—and the best single comment I have ever heard on the issue—she simply said: 'Well, Richard, you must understand: when a place gets boring, even the rich people leave.'"[13] Leaving Florida and his theories aside, this exchange testifies to Jacobs' confidence in the salutary effects of deregulation. It would be a stretch to suggest that she had a direct role in shaping the current condo boom, but today's Toronto, where developers are usually calling the shots, is more or less consistent with the kind of city Jacobs endorsed.

11.
Lang, Glenna and Marjory Wunsch, *Genius of Common Sense: Jane Jacobs and the Story of The Death and Life of Great American Cities*. Boston: David R. Godine, 2009: 35. Print.

12.
This reference to Adam Smith is appropriate, given Jacobs' interest in economy. After *The Death and Life*, she published several books that dealt with cities and economy; however, none of them garnered the same degree of praise her blockbuster debut did. Her perspective on cities and economy is succinctly summarized by Charles Abrams: "She ignores or slights such important influences on the urban economy as location, basic resources, climate, transportation, availability of skills, differential wage rates, the impact of government policy, particularly taxation and subsidies, public development strategies and other factors that speed or retard urban growth. Her theory is put forth in a kind of vacuum in which cities grow and wane in accordance with her few and simple rules." Abrams, Charles. "The Economy Of Cities," *The New York Times*, 1 June 1969. Web.

13.
Florida, Richard. "Getting Jane Jacobs Right." *The Atlantic*, 2 April 2010. Web.

14.
Myers, Barton. "Intro-
duction," Design
*Quarterly 108: Vacant
Lottery.* Minneapolis:
Walker Art Center,
1978: 7. Print.

15.
In 1997, the
Toronto-based Jane
Jacobs Prize was
created, and one year
after her death in
2006, she was fully
canonized with the
establishment of the
annual Jane's Walks,
neighbourhood pro-
cessions that are now
held in many different
cities during the first
weekend of May,
close to her birthday.

16.
Baird, George.
*Writings on Archi-
tecture and the
City.* London: Artifice,
2015: 106. Print.

Urbanity

A much more sophisticated critique of the conventional planning methods characteristic of the protohistory of the condo tower came from architects George Baird, Barton Myers, and Jack Diamond. From the mid-70s onward, Baird worked on the formulation of his postmodern ideas about the city. He published *onbuildingdowntown: Design Guidelines for the Core Area*, whose title's syntax reflects the argument for higher density. Baird also contributed an article to Vacant Lottery, a special issue of *Design Quarterly* published by the Walker Art Centre in Minneapolis that he co-edited with Myers. *Vacant Lottery* was the duo's "low-rise manifesto," which outlined "a philosophy of urban consolidation, an approach to urban development in opposition to the currently pervasive uni-centred high density/high-rise North American city with its sprawling suburban periphery...to propose an attitude that might return to our cities an urbanity they once had, effecting a reconciliation of good design and social commitment."[14] Vacant Lottery was dedicated to Jacobs, an early sign of the beatification that occurred during her lifetime; however, it is hard to reconcile given the difference between the nuanced and broad views of Baird and Myers and the shortsightedness of Jacobs'.[15]

In an introduction to a recent reprint of *Vacant Lottery*, Baird describes how in the 1970s he "became increasingly interested in the architectural tendency that came to be known as European Rationalism—in its Italian mode even often called simply 'the Tendenza.'"[16] This became the inspiration for *Vacant Lottery*. Even though it was impossible to translate the rationalism of Rossi and Ungers one-to-one to Toronto, the idea of urbanity, this *je ne sais quoi* that makes many European cities such great places, took hold in the city, albeit less in the shape of built forms and more so as laments of what the city was missing and dearly needed. Urbanity is professional jargon to describe places that are both

urban and urbane. This ideal state of the city is apparently hard to achieve in modernist environments in which buildings are floating in space; it works better when urbanites are more snugly surrounded by built substance. Reduced to its simplest reading, Myers and Baird's *Vacant Lottery* is a plea to fill voids as the first prerequisite to making Toronto more urban and urbane. However, there is a haunting "Doomsday" scenario looming in the background of their text, represented in a 'what if' diagram that shows the St. Jamestownization of much of downtown. *Vacant Lottery* was prescient in two ways. Vacant sites, which, once upon a time, were frequently parking lots, were the first plots to be built upon. These developments have made the city more urban and have undeniably generated some of the urbanity they believed would make Toronto a better place. At the same time, the Doomsday scenario they wanted to avoid is currently playing out, albeit not in the form of the St. Jamestownization they predicted, but in a pervasive condominiumization. The caption for the original Doomsday image read: "This 'Doomsday' depicts a section of Toronto realized according to Toronto's official plans if there were no bylaws to permit alternatives."[17] Sherbourne Lanes, a housing project by Myers and Diamond, was the lodestar of this manifestly low-rise alternative, which was tellingly explained in *Vacant Lottery* with an illustration of a skyscraper turned 90 degrees, lying on its side. It goes without saying that the current state of urbanity has in fact become the opposite: it obeys the logic of the felled skyscraper resurrected.

Unleashed Forces

When modern high-rises and the elevated Gardiner Expressway were planned, they were seen as a pretty decent way of dealing with certain acute problems of the city. Today there is a tendency to consider them grave errors. But it needs to be pointed out

17.
Myers, Barton. "Urban Consolidation," *Design Quarterly 108: Vacant Lottery*. Minneapolis: Walker Art Center, 1978: 11. Print.

18.
This paraphrases
a cartoon from the
1960s by Swedish
architect Mats Erik
Molander. In the
cartoon a planner is
overlooking a city
and says: "We must
replace our old errors
with up-to-date ones."

that politicians and planners continue to promulgate the same delusion: that they will do it better than their predecessors. Without denying the possibility of progress, history has shown time and again that politics and planning are particularly prone to fixing mistakes of the past by creating new ones.[18] One does not have to be clairvoyant to foresee that the swift and unyielding condominiumization of Toronto has all the right ingredients to become a recipe for the future's past mistake on a scale that will likely dwarf the Gardiner.

Some people might be quick to point out a fundamental difference between the sweeping effects of modernization on Toronto of the 1950s and 60s and the equally, if not even more wholesale, sweeping effects of the condo boom on the city today. The former represented a top-down product wrought by municipal city planning, and the latter, while not necessarily bottom-up (although that is obviously how towers get built), is nevertheless the product of an allegedly free market. Yet, their impact on the city continues to be very similar. Back then there was a belief that all that was needed was clear policy to steer the direction of urban development, whereas presently it seems that the city is developing with little hard policy guiding the way. Popular opposition was possible in the 1960s because there were identifiable public institutions and politicians to oppose and hold accountable. Nowadays, with the advent of developer-driven urbanization, there are more moving pieces and targets. Developers have a huge impact on city life, but they are not elected officials who can be ousted in an election. Moreover, the approval process has become more opaque, and the negotiation of each new building proposal depends largely on relationships among the different parties and Section 37 barters. Even if one is willing to believe that projects like the Gardiner Expressway or the aborted Spadina Expressway were the products of too much government planning, the current overdose of condo towers isn't necessarily a strong counterargument for leaving everything in the hands of the free market.

Yet, despite the indifferent uniformity of all of its towers, Toronto has become a very lively city, and according to all kinds of rankings it turns out to be a very livable place as well. To see how much it has changed—or, according to some, improved—it suffices to take a look at pictures of Toronto's streetscape before the 1990s, which now seems barely recognizable. At street level, today's Toronto has become a completely different place, with its fancy stores, hip bars, and cool restaurants, all part and parcel of a rapid gentrification process. Former Toronto mayor Barbara Hall deserves credit for enabling the latter, as Christopher Hume describes in the *Toronto Star*: "In the few years she presided over the old Toronto (1994 to '97), she made changes that enriched the city by billions of dollars and continue to do so today. Though few are aware, or care, it was Hall who initiated the 'two Kings' policy that brought new life—social, cultural, and economic—to then shabby parts of the downtown core. Simply by eliminating outdated zoning regulations and replacing them with new rules focused on mixed uses and built form, she unleashed forces that have remade the face of Toronto."[19]

Even though Hall's intervention focused chiefly on King Street, her approach became a template for other parts of downtown as well. This unleashing of forces opened a Pandora's box, ultimately leading to the rise and sprawl of condo towers everywhere. Despite the free rein given to development, it is striking to note that above street level, this freedom hasn't translated into heterogeneity. Tellingly, the colour spectrum of all the Identikit towers ranges from greenish grey to greyish green to greyish beige. The absence of vivid colours is commensurate with the near absence of any memorable formal expression beyond the obvious verticality of the

19.
Myers, Barton. "Urban Consolidation," *Design Quarterly 108: Vacant Lottery*. Minneapolis: Walker Art Center, 1978: 11. Print.

20.
Tall Building Design Guidelines. Toronto: City of Toronto, 2013: 5.

towers. In this respect there is a huge gap between the built reality and the municipal wishes as formulated in the 2013 edition of the *Tall Building Design Guidelines*: "Regardless of stylistic approach, the design and placement of all tall buildings should make a positive contribution to the public realm, fit harmoniously within the surrounding context and skyline."[20] Not many will deny that it is hard to find any condo tower in Toronto that approximates even a degree of these ambitions.

But this isn't necessarily a problem. The character of many cities is not determined by a few monumental buildings. Of course, Paris has the Eiffel Tower, the Louvre, and much more, but the typical image of the city is a tree-lined boulevard with cream-coloured apartment buildings. Many of them have the names of the architect discreetly chiseled in the stone façade, but nearly none of those is a household name. The architects are not well known, but the architecture isn't anonymous.

In a bit more than a decade, the condo tower has become a defining element of Toronto's cityscape. And with all the building proposals in the pipeline, it will become even more so in the next ten years. This makes it Toronto's equivalent of the Haussmannian apartment building. Yet, there are some crucial differences: while the Parisian apartment building has proven to be versatile, the condo tower doesn't seem to offer much space for different usages over time. But more importantly, while the apartment block in Paris is uniquely Parisian, the condo tower of Toronto isn't. So far, the condo tower is, to paraphrase the title of Robert Musil's famous novel, "an architecture without qualities." A Parisian apartment building is instantly recognizable as Parisian. Unfortunately, this isn't true for the typical condo tower in Toronto. It is no coincidence that so many renderings and photos of condo towers have the CN Tower somewhere in the background. Without it, nobody would be able to tell where they were.

CATALOGUE

ELEMENTS OF CONDO ARCHITECTURE

PARTISANS

What follows is a catalogue that is both a record of Toronto's condo boom as well as an examination of the condo object itself. It is an attempt to distill the headiness of the rise and sprawl phenomenon and break it down into its elemental pieces. Equal parts vernacular taxonomy and delamination, the catalogue asserts the importance of a close reading of the condo building as both object and commodity.

As an architectural object, the condominium tends to be generic and relatively unremarkable; however, the buildings embody a complex web of values and trends that make them more fascinating than they might initially appear. Condos and all their component parts "speak"—they at once conceal and reveal competing interests and pressures. There is an obsessive, sometimes myopic, attention paid to condos—everyone has a stake in or an opinion about Toronto's boom. The catalogue seeks to readjust that focal length by anatomizing the parts to reframe the whole.

To redress the latter, the catalogue aims as much as possible at a neutral dissection of condos into their constituent parts. The buildings and their components are presented independent of their physical, social, and commercial contexts to bring greater attention to their architectural qualities and branded representations. Thus, the catalogue surveys scale, dimension, division, placement, arrangement, orientation, and articulation, as well as a variety of hard and soft elements, from building forms, units, and colour swatches, to statistics, renderings, and public art projects. Importantly, nothing is inert; everything is underwritten by a host of forces ranging from entrepreneurial, political, architectural, and technological, to demographic, aspirational, psycho-spatial, and pragmatic.

It bears remembering that condominiums are frequently referred to as "products." Baked into these commodities are use and exchange values as well as relationships among various stakeholders: owners, tenants, investors, neighbours, community leaders, real estate agents, marketing teams, developers, politicians, architects, interior designers, engineers, consultants, planners, construction workers, project managers, and inspectors. The efforts made to average out all the competing needs and interests of so many different players may in fact be why the resultant towers end up being so stubbornly average.

In proportion to the scale of the boom, the scale of the city, and the scale of the condos themselves, the modest scale of the catalogue is hopelessly incommensurate. What is out of proportion in quantity is reconciled here with a curated taxonomy. Selective yet diverse, the catalogue attempts to present an unbiased, representative sample from a frenzied period of condo development in Toronto from 2004 onwards. It includes built, proposed, under-construction, and unrealized projects from every year during the boom and all areas of the city: from downtown and midtown to the waterfront and the suburbs, including Etobicoke, Scarborough, North York, and Mississauga, no region has been untouched. There are buildings marketed and priced for a variety of demographics, driven by numerous developers, and designed by scads of architects. Major players with the biggest physical impact and longest track records make the most appearances.

STATE OF THE BOOM

Condos both create and respond to numerous macro demographic
and economic conditions, a few of which are chronicled here.

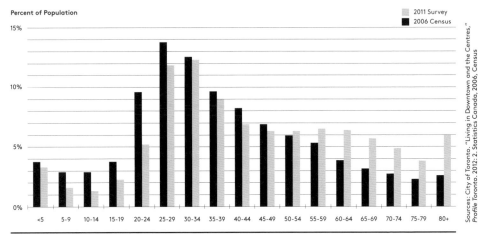

Percent of Population

2011 Survey
2006 Census

Sources: City of Toronto. "Living in Downtown and the Centres,"
Profile Toronto. 2012; 2. Statistics Canada, 2006, Census

AGE STRUCTURE IN DOWNTOWN AND THE CENTRES

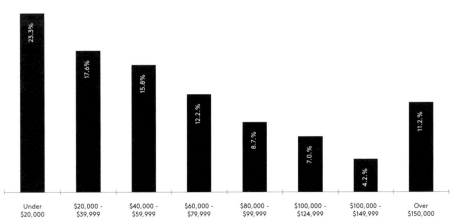

Sources: Oatler, Thomas. *Downtown Toronto: Trends,
Issues, Intensification.* City of Toronto, 2014; 25.

PERCENT DOWNTOWN HOUSEHOLDS BY INCOME (2010)

Retrofit of Multi-Unit Residential Buildings in Cold Climates.
Toronto: University of Toronto, 2009: 7.

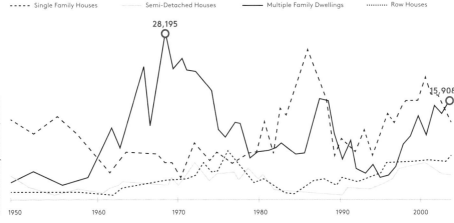

- - - - Single Family Houses ·········· Semi-Detached Houses ——— Multiple Family Dwellings ·········· Row Houses

28,195

15,908

1950 1960 1970 1980 1990 2000

HOUSING STARTS IN GREATER TORONTO AREA, 1950-2005

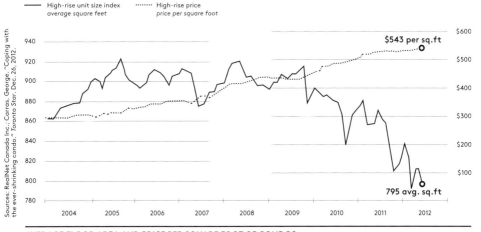

——— High-rise unit size index
average square feet   ·········· High-rise price
price per square foot

$543 per sq.ft

795 avg. sq.ft

2004 2005 2006 2007 2008 2009 2010 2011 2012

Sources: RealNet Canada Inc.; Carras, George. "Coping with
the ever-shrinking condo." Toronto Star. Dec. 26, 2012.

**AVERAGE FLOOR AREA AND PRICE PER SQUARE FOOT OF CONDOS
IN THE GREATER TORONTO AREA, 2004–2005**

ARCHITECTS AND DEVELOPERS

This diagram delineates relationships between architects and developers on a total of 388 proposed, completed, or to be completed projects in Toronto (2006-2019). This diagram is not exhaustive; major players with the biggest impact and longest track records make the most appearances.

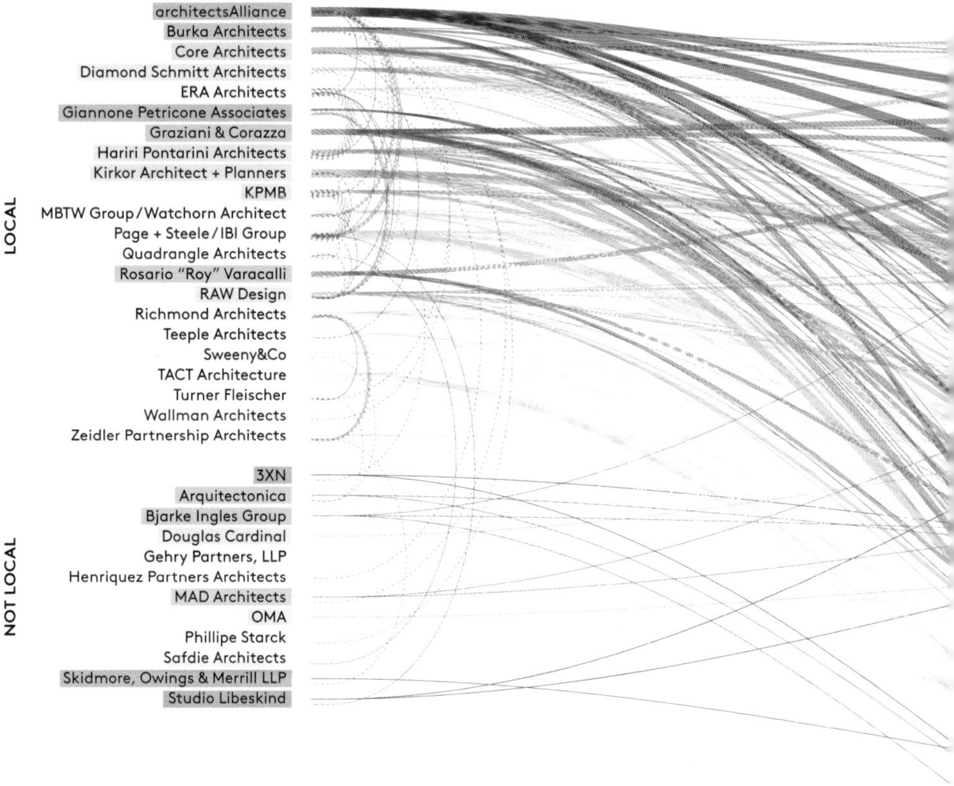

LOCAL

architectsAlliance
Burka Architects
Core Architects
Diamond Schmitt Architects
ERA Architects
Giannone Petricone Associates
Graziani & Corazza
Hariri Pontarini Architects
Kirkor Architect + Planners
KPMB
MBTW Group / Watchorn Architect
Page + Steele / IBI Group
Quadrangle Architects
Rosario "Roy" Varacalli
RAW Design
Richmond Architects
Teeple Architects
Sweeny&Co
TACT Architecture
Turner Fleischer
Wallman Architects
Zeidler Partnership Architects

NOT LOCAL

3XN
Arquitectonica
Bjarke Ingles Group
Douglas Cardinal
Gehry Partners, LLP
Henriquez Partners Architects
MAD Architects
OMA
Phillipe Starck
Safdie Architects
Skidmore, Owings & Merrill LLP
Studio Libeskind

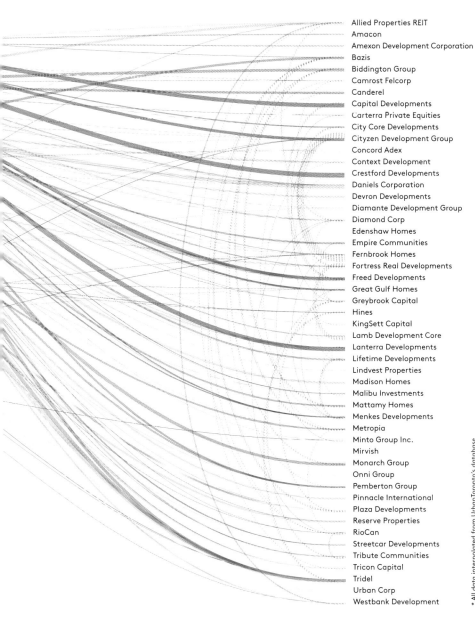

Allied Properties REIT
Amacon
Amexon Development Corporation
Bazis
Biddington Group
Camrost Felcorp
Canderel
Capital Developments
Carterra Private Equities
City Core Developments
Cityzen Development Group
Concord Adex
Context Development
Crestford Developments
Daniels Corporation
Devron Developments
Diamante Development Group
Diamond Corp
Edenshaw Homes
Empire Communities
Fernbrook Homes
Fortress Real Developments
Freed Developments
Great Gulf Homes
Greybrook Capital
Hines
KingSett Capital
Lamb Development Core
Lanterra Developments
Lifetime Developments
Lindvest Properties
Madison Homes
Malibu Investments
Mattamy Homes
Menkes Developments
Metropia
Minto Group Inc.
Mirvish
Monarch Group
Onni Group
Pemberton Group
Pinnacle International
Plaza Developments
Reserve Properties
RioCan
Streetcar Developments
Tribute Communities
Tricon Capital
Tridel
Urban Corp
Westbank Development

* All data interpolated from UrbanToronto's database

PLAYERS – ARCHITECTS

How the condo architects describe themselves
The following architecture firms have played a significant part in Toronto's post-2000 condo boom. All descriptions are taken from each firm's respective website (April 2016).

architectsAlliance

aA is a design-driven studio. We encourage fresh thinking, honest questions and tough decisions. We work collaboratively: every member of a project team—including our client—has a voice. A core team, led by our Principal and one or more Associates, is assigned to each project, to ensure ultimate accountability and responsive day-by-day stewardship of our clients' goals. Our collaborative approach extends to the composition of our project teams: aA has collaborated with other architects in Canada, the US and Europe; lab and LEED® consultants in the US and Germany; and engineers in cities across Canada. In design as in nature, cross-pollination breeds strength, diversity and innovation.

Burka Architects Inc.

The architectural practice was established in 1971 with the objective of full partici-pation in the rapidly evolving urban archi-tecture and human habitation of the modern city. To this end, this office pursues excellence in design through respect for use, function, form, economy, context and environment as well as style in all of its building designs. This office recognizes that buildings are a reflection of their time and the architect is the interpreter of these relevant expressions...
The firm's innovative designs have substantially influenced the overall condo-minium market and left permanent and recognizable standard features in Toronto area projects. This office perceives the concept of any good project to be rooted in the existing physical and cultural context as well as in the marketplace specific to its area. Hence, the building

form, the site layout and the unit layout is a direct result of a dialogue between marketing experts, the parameters of zoning restrictions, construction costs and design efficiency consideration and appropriate "architectural style" for its context. Our ultimate programmatic objective is to maximize the total "sales value" of the project. This means more than just monetary value; it means value to be builder, the purchasers and in a wider context to society at large.

CORE Architects Inc.

CORE Architects Inc. is an award-winning group of architects and interior designers based in Toronto. Since our formation in 1994, we have quickly distinguished our-selves amongst our competitors by our innovative yet thoughtful design solutions. The firm's founding principals, Babak Eslahjou, Charles Gane, and Deni Poletti share a design philosophy that focuses on creativity, innovation and sustainability; and a business vision that is client-focused, striving to maximize efficiency while meet-ing schedule and budgetary constraints.

Diamond Schmitt Architects

When it comes to the buildings designed by Diamond Schmitt Architects, ours is a first principle approach. Whether the project is a small and simple structure or a large and complex facility, we always begin with the client goals, a thorough program review, an analysis of the site and contextual considerations, and an evaluation of all credible planning and design options.
In addition, our approach to design includes a significant social dimension:

the informal interaction that is of immense benefit to multi-disciplinary institutions, the quality of place that attracts the best researchers and students to campus facilities, or the sense of occasion that enhances attendance at performing arts buildings. Our designs are shaped to ensure the achievement of such outcomes.

We believe that architecture that is environmentally responsible is of prime importance. Our commitment to sustainability and green design is demonstrated in our thirty architects on staff that are LEED (Leadership in Energy and Environmental Design) accredited, and the many awards we have received in the advancement of sustainable systems and technologies. Our unique approach to architecture is that of true economy in construction, taking both capital and operating costs into account. For both practical and ethical considerations, sustainability has always been a central principle of our design approach.

Our practice has, as a consequence, established new benchmarks in this field.

ERA Architects

Our core interest is in connecting heritage to wider considerations of urban design and city building, and to a larger set of cultural values that provide perspective to our work at every scale. Our core values are in generating professional integrity and expertise through research, education and mentoring. To that end ERA frequently works collaboratively with other firms to engage in city building, conserving heritage architecture and improving the built environment. We also generate publications and exhibitions related to Toronto and to Canada's built environment.

E.I. Richmond Architects

E.I. Richmond Architects Ltd. is a medium-sized architectural firm specializing in large as well as small-scale condominium residences, retail, commercial and institutional buildings. The company has operated in Toronto since 1992 and has been a leading architectural firm for some of the city's most impressive high rise buildings.

At the heart of E.I. Richmond's practice are both its design and technical teams. These are led by senior architects who report directly to the principals in charge of the project. The developing schemes are subject to regular Design Reviews within the office to ensure that quality is maintained. Clients receive dedicated, personalized service and accountability.

From strategic site planning and investigation to the design and approval process. E.I. Richmond Architects Ltd. staff handles every aspect of architectural development with efficiency, expertise and creativity.

Giannone Petricone Associates

While retaining elemental simplicity and restraint, Giannone Petricone Associates' projects delight in their acknowledgement of the city at all scales, and their simultaneously practical and emotive transformation of spaces, surfaces and details. The work evokes a love of modernism mixed with a genuine sense of joy in the unexpected, imbuing projects with both intellectual and sensorial pleasure. Dedicated to design excellence and client service, Giannone Petricone Associates approaches each project with a collaborative spirit, uniting curiosity, research and skill in planning and architecture with a thorough understanding of locality, client requirements and ambitions, and tectonic possibilities. Partnerships with manufacturers and craftspeople result in innovative forms and materials. The resulting projects are imaginative, responsive and beautifully crafted.

Grazini + Corazza Architcts Inc.

Established in 1997, Graziani + Corazza's fusion of architectural vision and experience is tailor-made to create the singular and iconic. At the core of this Toronto-based architectural practice lies a corporate philosophy dedicated to viewing each and every project on its own merits and then pushing the creative envelope to ensure the most unique and dynamic solution. Small or large, residential or commercial, mixed use community, institutional icon or neighbourhood infill, our dedication to achieving a fresh architectural response to our client's brief informs our reputation.

Hariri Pontarini Architects

Hariri Pontarini Architects is a full-service Canadian firm devoted to producing work of lasting value. Siamak Hariri and David Pontarini founded the Toronto office in 1994 motivated by a shared commitment to design quality. Today their 70-person practice offers its clients in-depth partner involvement through all stages of design and the breadth of building experience and technical expertise to rigorously oversee construction. HPA believes solid relationships result in strong projects. They take

pride in forging lasting collaborations with all involved in the design, development and construction process: clients, consultants, fabricators, policymakers, construction workers, colleagues. With each commission, HPA assumes full responsibility to materialize a design vision inspiring to its occupants, attuned to its setting and respectful of stakeholder needs, client budget and timeline. Every project in their diversely scaled, award-winning portfolio reflects the HPA mission to craft architectural and urban solutions that exceed expectations, without excess.

Kirkor Architects & Planners

Kirkor's focus is on the creation of responsible, sustainable, economically viable developments through smart growth strategies. We have expertise in urban design principles of intensification, mixed-use development and public transportation that are necessary to ensure holistic, healthy building practices. Urban intensification is a critical issue for cities that must cope with rising populations while curbing sprawl. Kirkor is an authority in urban densification with award-winning smart build projects across North America.

KPMB Architects

KPMB Architects is an award winning, internationally recognized Canadian practice. It is notable for its unique hybrid form of architecture and practice, developed to respond to our multi-cultural, dynamically changing world. This is manifested in the diversity of the portfolio for culture, education, healthcare and paradigm shifting climate responsive design. Every project is conceived to support an essential belief in the power of architecture to influence civil and moral conditions. The firm comprises a deep pool of highly talented women and men who together form dynamic integrated design teams to ensure every design solution balances vision and pragmatism, environmentally responsible design and architectural excellence.

MBTW Group / Watchorn Architect
Since 1975, The MBTW Group / W Architect Inc. has been creating distinctive, innovative "places for people", and is recognized as a leader in the urban design, landscape architecture, architecture, design guidance, golf and leisure design industry. The firm has designed numerous, award-winning parks, public spaces, innovative new communities and mixed-use projects. Our collective experience spans local, national and international markets.
There's a synergy within our 60-strong team, as we co-ordinate planning, architecture and landscape architecture to find unique design solutions for specific challenges. In order to create a strong sense of place, the firm works closely with clients to establish strong project identity with distinctive character.
In the realm of urban design, we are experts in visioning, designing and implementing innovative new communities. Landscape architecture at MBTW is about the understanding and creation of highly animated and successful open spaces. Our passion for excellence is consistent when applied to street systems, city blocks, waterfronts, parks, urban plazas and natural systems.

Page + Steele / IBI Group Architects
Founded in 1926, Page + Steele has established an award winning tradition of excellence and professionalism. The firm has recently became a subsidiary of IBI Group, a multidisciplinary global practice headquartered in Toronto, and is now known as Page + Steele / IBI Group Architects (P+S / IBI). The firm has extensive expertise in the design of hotel, residential, office and retail uses. P+S / IBI's experience in these areas has led to the emergence of the firm as the pre-eminent Canadian firm engaged in the design of mixed-use developments. Our reputation for hotel and residential design has led P+S / IBI to many Canadian and International commissions and projects for some of the largest developers in North America and best known international hotel brands.

Quadrangle Architects
At Quadrangle, we balance creative innovation with in-depth expertise to solve business challenges—and build lasting partnerships. We collaborate with high-profile clients in media, hospitality, retail and other sectors, as well as developers of multi-unit residential projects. Our Toronto-based firm includes recognized leaders in areas such as accessibility and sustainable design, as well as experts in technically demanding industries such as Content Media. Over the years, our work has earned acclaim and won many Canadian and international awards. That recognition is gratifying, but what we value most is the strength it adds to existing relationships and the doors it opens to new ones. Maintaining our

focus comes down (as usual) to four simple rules: Never rest on our laurels. Never talk when we can act. Never stop learning. And, most important, never stop evolving—as we keep pace with the changing world where our clients grow businesses, build communities and create new opportunities.

RAW Design

Unconcerned with stylistic expectations, RAW architecture focuses on understanding of site opportunities and client specific objectives. Evolving from a critical investigation of site and context and filtered through an imaginative design process we develop clear concepts which become strong urban form. We take a completely open-minded approach to architecture, encouraging a fluid and collaborative design process.

r. Varacalli Architect Inc

r. Varacalli Architect inc. is a Toronto architectural firm creating buildings that are integral to the city fabric, that is, buildings that belong to the street, to the neighbourhood, to the skyline, and to the city. Buildings constructed on under-utilized city blocks, to revitalize and intensify existing neighbourhoods, taking the opportunity of street life, public transit and neighbourhood amenities. Buildings designed to be sustainable.
Buildings that are designed to have an array of mixed uses. Street retail, podium floors with office spaces, and residential apartments above.
Buildings designed to be constructed of conventional materials, arranged in a re-adaptive composition.
Buildings designed to understand economic sensibilities.
Buildings designed to be memorable, poetic and artful.

Sweeney&Co Architects Inc.

Sweeny&Co is a Toronto-based multi-disciplinary architecture, design and real estate consultancy. Started in 1987 by Dermot Sweeny, we design measurably better places that are healthy and comfortable to live, work, learn and play in. We are known for our award-winning sustainable architecture that promotes design excellence for both urban and suburban environment.
Dermot Sweeny, John Gillanders and Caroline Richard lead the firm's core competencies in commercial and residential and institutional architecture which are built upon:
– Advocating for the "better build" smart design model, which champions innovative ways to build adaptable, flexible, more humane and measurably better environments and;
– Leading the way in sustainable design ideas, continually participating in the global initiative to improve the environment and minimize the negative impact on the planet.

TACT Architecture Inc.

The success of TACT Architecture inherently lies in our ability to work with our Clients to achieve noteworthy architecture while meeting tight financial constraints and achieving optimal density. We do not treat cost efficiency as a separate issue; instead, it is integrated into our criteria from the beginning of the design process. This approach, and the efficiency and creativity with which we apply it, helps to distinguish us from other firms and turns our first time clients into repeat clients. TACT Architecture is headed by Principal Prishram Jain, whose distinctive sense of design and extensive working knowledge of the development industry, inform all of the firm's work.

Turner Fleischer

Turner Fleischer builds for the future with tools, technology and knowledge of tomorrow's world. We embrace change, new thoughts, technology and, where we see great benefits to all, we run with it. This progressive philosophy can be seen in our firm's dedication to sustainable design. No vision, however, can come to fruition without the full understanding and approval of the client, municipality and community. To this end, we create and present every project through sophisticated 3D visualizations to evoke its full dimensions and potential.

Wallman Architects

We offer in-depth partner involvement during design and municipal approvals and are recognized for our ability to operate within demanding bureaucratic and political environments. Working collaboratively, our team of experienced professionals ensures the successful completion of all project phases from design to construction, within the client's budget and timelines. We value the long-term relationships that we have developed with clients, consultants, contractors and co-workers.
Each commission enriches the lives of its occupants, is environmentally sustainable

and embodies a unique design vision. We embrace the complexities of architectural practice and seek to unlock its potential to enhance the value of the built environment.

Zeidler Partnership Architects

Zeidler Partnership Architects is a full service firm providing master planning, functional planning, and architectural and interior design services. With our decades of practice in Ontario and internationally, Zeidler has seen hundreds of buildings through from concept to completion. Our portfolio of work exemplifies accessible, sustainable, and evidence-based design through an integrated delivery process. We combine years of experience with the input of clients and collaborators to produce an ongoing portfolio of work that includes civic and academic buildings, commercial and residential properties, healthcare and research facilities, performing arts centres, and hotels and resorts. In addition to the traditional design-bid-build approach, we have successfully completed projects in numerous construction delivery methods, and have served in both compliance and proponent roles in major Public-Private Partnership (P3) infrastructure projects for DBF and DBFM projects.
We dedicate one partner to lead our team through each project and ensure expert continuity. Our approach integrates the partner's personal and creative vision with the varied and complementary expertise of our team. Our longstanding reputation is founded on the successful and fiscally responsible completion of our buildings, as well as on their enduring quality.

PLAYERS – DEVELOPERS

How the condo developers describe themselves
The following developers have played a significant part in Toronto's post-2000 condo boom.
All descriptions are taken from each developer's respective website (April 2016).

Amacon

Driven by a passion for detail and a tradition of excellence in design and architecture, Amacon is recognized as one of Canada's most influential real estate development and construction firms. Amacon's vision is to continue to be one of Canada's largest and most successful builders for decades to come. Laying the foundation with excellence today, Amacon controls all aspects of the development process including: Site Acquisition, Project Design, Development, Construction, Marketing and Sales. With four decades of development and construction expertise, a precise level of design and craftsmanship is evident in all the homes and commercial developments that Amacon builds. To create a product with long-term value, it is imperative to understand a customer's wants and needs. With ongoing market research, Amacon is able to provide a product that is both innovative and functional.

At Amacon, our dedication to service and customer care stands behind everything we build. All new Amacon homes are backed by a 2/5/10 warranty, the most comprehensive third party coverage in North America, if not the world. And our knowledgeable staff's commitment to excellence includes superior after sales customer care, earning Amacon the loyalty of thousands of satisfied homeowners over the years.

Amexon Development Corporation

With a proven history spanning over 35 years and a remarkable record of success in commercial and luxury condominium developments, Amexon has established an outstanding reputation in the industry, striving to create vibrant developments and communities employing cutting edge design.

We draw on an integrated team of professionals with diverse technical discipline and construction backgrounds to offer our clients a quality product and comprehensive after-sales service.

Our excellent performance record, tradition of superior construction and responsiveness provides our clients and investors the assurance of consistent quality and professional service.

Combining a unique balance of development experience and local market knowledge has earned us an esteemed reputation in all facets of the real estate development industry.

Averton Homes

At Averton, we are committed to our audiences. A home is much more than bricks and sticks. We believe that a home is safety, comfort and security.

A home is the place where we become the people we want to be and build the lives that we have always imagined. Our home matters. Every house that Averton builds is rooted in a strong foundation. Mixed in with our concrete are the values that drive us as a family to build the best we can: integrity, professionalism, and personal service. We know that if we get our part right, it's going to help families across Canada to build a better life. Averton builds communities and homes where people can live happy and fulfilling lives. We present solutions that meet the needs of everyone involved along the way. As a market leader in both Eastern and Western Canada, we are a proven resource, and a trusted solution. Averton invests time and resources at every stage of development. Everything we do is a considered process, and everything revolves around our audience. This means we use quality materials, proven construction techniques, and innovative technology. We are an industry leader thanks to our principles of design and innovation in everything we do.

Biddington Group

Good design is timeless. Couple it with the finest building materials, expert construction and superior property management, and you've got Biddington.

The Biddington Group of Companies is a respected family-owned enterprise whose origins date back to the early 60s and whose dedication to quality and service is exemplary.

Over the years, Biddington has developed numerous high-rise communities – both rental and condominium—as well as neighbourhoods of luxurious single family homes, in Ontario and the southeastern United States.

Today The Biddington Group, in addition to their home building division, also owns and manages an extensive portfolio of more than two million square feet of industrial, commercial and residential units.

Canderel Stoneridge Equity Group

Canderel's success as a multi-faceted real estate development, management and asset management company is a reflection of the company's exceptionally high standards and desire to exceed customer and partner expectations. The Canderel team is comprised of the industry's top talent, having an innovative vision combined with the will and resources to get the job done on time and on budget. Ours is a disciplined, focused, creative and flexible approach that has consistently provided unparalleled value and service. Over the years, we have developed a set of core competencies and operating principles to ensure this is achieved.

Capital Developments

Capital Developments is an industry leading Canadian real estate development company, with international roots. We believe in finding partners that get it. Working with those that care as much as we do. And developing amazing projects with meaningful connections.

With years of experience, we've learned that architecture, location, interior design, glass, metal and concrete all matter. But we've also learned that personal connections, trust and relationships are the things we really build

City-Core Developments

City-Core Development is an integrated real estate operating and investment management company. We invest in urban infill mixed-use projects across the United States. Company projects often combine retail, commercial, hospitality and residential uses. Our projects—completed and underway—have an aggregate value exceeding $2 billion.

City-Core uses creative strategies to realize the value of underutilized, poorly marketed, and distressed assets—often transforming them into mixed-use buildings. Our approach leverages a national trend towards urban living. Since 1991,

City-Core has fulfilled a unique niche in real estate investment. The principals at City-Core have been working together for the past 18 years and collectively have more than 100 years of real estate and institutional investment management expertise. The Company is headquartered in San Francisco. City-Core or the "Company" is defined as City-Core Development, Inc. and all of its subsidiaries.

Cityzen Development Group

Cityzen is one of the Greater Toronto Area's most recognized builders with a passion for design. Our urban communities are highly sought after and our award-winning architects and designers are always pushing boundaries. Our mission is to make your community feel comfortable, convenient and refined.

Some of our notable partners include Yansong Ma, Daniel Libeskind, Munge Leung, Architects Alliance and Waterfront Toronto.

Concord Adex / Concord Pacific

Concord Pacific Group Inc. is a leading developer of urban, master-planned residential neighbourhoods that are purposefully designed to enhance the lifestyles of its residents. This Canadian company's first endeavour was Concord Pacific Place, a 204-acre residential/commercial development in Vancouver. Located along a strip of downtown waterfront that stretches for miles, it is the largest residential/commercial urban development currently being built in North America. Architects and city planners from around the world visiting Concord Pacific Place consider it a development form that

provides a vibrant, sustainable lifestyle welcomed by young professionals, families and empty nesters.

Context Developments

Context was formed in 1997 by Stephen Gross and Howard Cohen. Our company is focused on the development of mixed-use projects, condominiums and affordable rental housing in Toronto's central neighbourhoods. We are pioneers in downtown intensification with buildings based on quality design, sustainability and innovative city planning. Context is backed by Waterloo Capital, a private investment fund controlled by Stephen Gross and Gerald Schwartz, the CEO of Onex Corporation.

Cresford Developments

The first residential developer in Canada to dress up their condominiums with international fashion labels, Cresford is renowned for superb quality and attention to detail. Cresford condominiums feature inspirational living spaces that seamlessly flow from one to the next and sublime amenities that celebrate life and style. A trusted name in the market for over 40 years, a Cresford condominium inspires confidence and security.

Daniels Corporation

The Daniels Corporation builds with a passion for creating vibrant communities in every sense of the word. Daniels looks beyond the bricks and mortar, including social, cultural and economic infrastructures that will create a unique sense of place. This commitment has been an integral part of Daniels' corporate philosophy for over 30 years. Daniels has built more than 25,000 award-winning homes and apartments, master-planned mixed-use communities, and commercial and retail spaces, and has earned its standing as one of Canada's largest and preeminent builder/developers. Company founder John H. Daniels is a towering figure of the North American real estate industry. In a career that has spanned over 50 years, the former Chairman and CEO of Cadillac Fairview Development Corporation has left an indelible mark on the quality of the places in which people live, work, play, create and shop. Over the course of his career Mr. Daniels played a key role in the development of Canadian landmarks such as Toronto's Eaton Centre and Toronto-Dominion Centre, the 4,700 acre Erin Mills community in Mississauga and the brownfields reclamation of the Goodyear Tire Plant in Etobicoke.

Devron Developments

Devron Developments began as a family business in 1997. With a passion for architecture, engineering and sustainability, we strive to create well-crafted buildings that are equally beautiful and responsible. We pride ourselves in being long-term visionaries with a philosophy of benevolence and integrity; a practice we maintain on every detail from design through execution. With a longstanding reputation for high-quality customs homes, and in developing award winning condominiums, we are committed to creating liveable, thoughtfully designed homes that are built to last.

Edenshaw Homes

We build communities that you can call home. Our specialty is residential mid-to-high rise condominium communities in the City of Toronto and Greater Toronto Area.

Our commitment to the very best design, materials, and construction craftsmanship ensures that Edenshaw meets the very highest standards every time. Our focus is on building homes that last, in sustainable communities where families can forge the memories that last a lifetime.

This dedication to excellence stems from our core philosophy that buying a home is about more than just investing in property: it's about building a long-lasting connection to a community.

With a commitment to excellence, our talented and innovative team constantly strives to execute our vision of creating vibrant communities.

Fernbrook Homes

Architectural design innovation plays a major role in creating the Fernbrook difference. The company has a gift for choosing just the right style and incorporating flashes of brilliance amid a breathtaking tapestry of architectural excellence. This creative flair results in exceptional streetscapes and a distinguished ambience for both low-rise and high-rise communities. Whether it's steeply pitched Tudor gables, Chateau-style dormers and turrets, Regency stucco and columns, intricate Victorian trim work, or sleep glass-and-steel tower architecture, Fernbrook weaves meticulous details into facades that are individually striking, yet come together in perfect harmony. The effect is distinctively different and delightfully Fernbrook. Fernbrook communities are always graced with an atmosphere of exclusivity—a

Fernbrook neighbourhood embraces residents in a welcoming enclave, in the heart of a master planned community vision. Fernbrook's low-rise communities feature quiet crescents and cul-de-sacs, eliminating through traffic and creating a comfortable and safe neighbourhood for walking, bicycling and playing. Distinguished entry treatments introduce each community with an ambience that is unmistakably Fernbrook. Streetscapes showcase stylish exteriors designed with elegance and charm contributing both luxury and panche to their elegant settings. Homes that are sure to satisfy the most discerning tastes. Intimate and inviting, a community designed and built by Fernbook homes is truly "home" in every sense of the word.

Freed Developments
Building a lifestyle, that's the way we see it. Our business is about creating a way for people to enjoy living in a real community, close to where they work and play, in a building that makes a design statement. It's about living in a unique space designed to maximize natural light and urban views while facing a city park.
We're visionaries. Living in a building by Freed Developments might mean living in a reclaimed urban warehouse in the emerging downtown core, carefully restored and modernised to revitalise the cityscape. Or in a green, boxwood-wrapped eco-landmark, or a glass-walled, loft-inspired space with 10-foot ceilings above the Thompson boutique hotel and lifestyle complex. Or a building with a playful, avant-garde lobby designed by the globally acclaimed Philippe Starck.

Living the Freed lifestyle means the hottest sushi restaurant or hippest hotel lobby bar in town is just downstairs from your Toronto condo. Or if you're in Muskoka, having one of the best golf courses in the world right outside your front door. Our lifestyle provides everything you want out of life—in town, or country—to simply be part of your day-to-day routine.
Our vision means living better, by design. We believe that good design isn't just better-looking, it makes life better. Which is why Freed Developments doesn't just build condo units, we build architecture. Pure and simple, it's building—elevated from the ordinary—to become an expression of the way we want to live now.

Lanterra
Lanterra Developments started out with a vision to build iconic urban condominiums that offered a fine balance of location, luxury and lifestyle. Lanterra Developments was founded by Mark Mandelbaum and Barry Fenton, two real estate visionaries who began with a dream to develop innovative, one-of-a-kind downtown condominium properties. Within a short span of just 10 years, we have charted an amazing success story on the Toronto skyline with one iconic condominium after another, scaling new heights in design, style and elegant urban living. Our guiding philosophy goes beyond just condominium building to dynamic urban revitalization and putting Toronto on the global map as the new city of the future, with vibrant master planned mixed use communities, sustainable green living and cutting-edge environmental technologies.

Lifetime Developments

For more than three decades, Lifetime Developments has demonstrated unparalleled foresight, building in strategic locations across the Greater Toronto Area. By successfully identifying the neighbourhoods poised to become thriving communities, we remain at the forefront of the city's ever-burgeoning real estate industry. With our proven residential and commercial expertise we are creating unique spaces that invite you to live, work and dream. From conception to completion, Lifetime continues to set new benchmarks for design innovation and architectural excellence, exceeding expectations and inspiring new heights.

Lindvest Properties

A Toronto-based real estate development organization with deep roots, spanning six decades in the award-winning, highly-reputed H&R family of companies, Lindvest has designed and built diverse, successful developments in neighbourhoods and towns across the Greater Toronto Area.
As a company, Lindvest strives for excellence in all spheres of its business. Since our inception in 1998, we have been recognized for our excellence in planning, progressive urban design and high standards of construction, and have been successful in carving a niche in the competitive GTA new home market.
Another enduring value in the Lindvest universe is customer service. To fuel growth and success, we invest heavily in customer service. From the quality of our homes to our interactions with shoppers, buyers and owners, keeping you satisfied is paramount for us.

Whether it's a charming subdivision in a pristine setting or an iconic high-rise in the city, our award-wining communities are as vibrant and unique as the people who live in them. From convenient locations and beautiful settings to innovative designs and luxurious finishes, every detail of a Lindvest neighbourhood is rooted in our passion to help better your life.

Great Gulf Homes

Since 1975, the Great Gulf Group of Companies has grown from a regional home builder into one of North America's premier real estate organizations. With new projects underway in Canada and nine major U.S. cities from Atlanta to Denver, the company's fully integrated activities span the entire real estate spectrum. Master-planned communities and high-rise condominiums. Resort properties and conference centres. Office towers and shopping malls. All providing leading-edge design and state-of-the-art construction in prime locations. The company's "Live greatly" promise rises from our conviction that the world of property development and real estate is rapidly changing. Our commitment to three core values—Design, Technology, Customer Experience—reflects our determination to be instrumental in that transformation.

Minto

Minto's legacy of exceptional quality and craftsmanship is recognized industry-wide; however, we're most proud when we share the keys to wonderful memories at every stage of life. Whether it's the excitement of a first apartment, the possibilities of a second home to grow into, temporary housing while you're in transition or the accomplishment of an empty nest, Minto is there every step of the way. With operations in Ottawa, Toronto, Calgary, London and Florida—and plans to expand even further—our focus on what matters is apparent in every one of our apartments, furnished suites, homes, condominiums and commercial spaces. We've changed a great deal since our early days, but one thing that remains the same is our commitment to creating better places.

Monarch Group

Peter Jorgesen, son of a reputable homebuilder, established his own residential construction company Monarch Framing in 2005. Since that time, Monarch Framing expanded its focus to include commercial and condominium framing as well as residential and commercial wood structure modifications and renovations. Monarch Framing's projects include over three hundred single and multi-family homes for major homebuilders in Edmonton, as well as local landmarks such as the Edmonton Armories, and M-Trac buildings in downtown Edmonton.

Monarch Framing has since evolved into Monarch Group of Companies, and services have expanded to include homebuilding, specializing on infill builds in mature neighbourhoods. Monarch Group's team includes designers trained in lifespan and adaptable environments. Because of Monarch Group's experience and expertise, Monarch Homes are designed and built with economy, efficiency, and comfortable living for any stage in life.

Onni Group

The Onni Group is one of North America's leading private real estate developers, with extensive experience designing, developing, building and managing innovative projects. As a fully integrated company that directly oversees every step in the development process, Onni has built over 6,000 homes in the past decade. In addition, the company owns and manages 6.5 million square feet of commercial property and over 4,600 rental apartment units. With offices in Vancouver, Toronto, Chicago, Los Angeles, Phoenix and Mexico, Onni continues to expand and diversify into new markets throughout North America.

Pemberton Group

Over decades, Pemberton has built its reputation for creating successful residential and commercial developments of uncompromising quality. A Pemberton condominium rises above the rest because of the dedication, talent and leadership of the team behind it. Our residents benefit from design expertise and superb craftsmanship, and are surrounded by desirable features and truly exceptional amenities.

Plaza Developments

Since 1982, the Plaza philosophy of providing a uniformly high level of standard quality in every condominium Plaza builds has made our name synonymous with lasting value. We were among the first condominium developers and builders in Toronto to include such finishes as granite counters and floors, marble bathroom counters and floors, halogen lighting, under-mount sinks, porcelain tile, engineered hardwood floors and stainless steel appliances as standard features rather than costly upgrades. Building in more quality from the beginning is a hallmark of every Plaza community, which has resulted in condominium suites that have greater market value today, and have lasting value for tomorrow.

Tridel

We've come a long way since Jack DelZotto, the founder of our company built our first home in 1934. We think it's important we introduce you to Jack because his strong belief in family, home and community is the bedrock for our entire organization. Jack was ahead of his time in a lot of things and a true innovator, who built the first apartment complex in 1961, featuring twin towers, a swimming pool, a recreation centre and landscaped grounds, the forerunner of today's modern condominium.

Our founders redefined what 'home' is. A home is more than its physical prop-erties of bricks and mortar. It is a lifestyle and a community that connects us to each other and our surroundings. This idea transformed the industry (and our world). What we started over five decades ago is now recognized as the most innovative, sustainable concept in building new homes and communities.

Today, Jack's three sons, Angelo, Elvio and Leo and their children have carried on the tradition of family values, and innovation. A tradition that inspires everyone who works or is connected to Tridel, to be a part of something great, something bigger than themselves and to make the world a better place.

Urbancorp

Urbancorp has built thriving new communities in other up-and-coming Toronto neighbourhoods. The Neighbour-hoods of Queen Street East is comprised of three stunning new home communities along the Queen Street East corridor. With locations in Riverdale, Leslieville and The Beach, The Neighbourhoods of Queen Street East bring a fresh, modern vibe to the urban renaissance currently underway in Toronto's east end.

In central Toronto, Urbancorp's The Neighbourhoods of Downsview Park is one of the City of Toronto's largest residential developments. Adjoining the newly redeveloped 300 acre Downsview Park, The Neighbourhoods of Downsview Park offers stylish, modern townhome living right in the heart of one of Toronto's hottest new urban hubs.

With easy access to TTC, York University, Humber River Regional Hospital, Yorkdale Mall, shopping and restaurants—not to mention hiking and cycling trails, sports and recreation facilities and more at Downsview Park—Urbancorp has once again set a new standard for distinctive urban living at The Neighbourhoods of Downsview Park.

With Val, Urbancorp continues its legacy of creating some of the most vibrant and innovative home and condominium communities in the GTA.

OBJECTS – POINT TOWERS

Point towers are tall buildings with small floor plates that commonly approximate square or round proportions. They often feature a podium comprised of townhomes or commercial spaces.

18 YORKVILLE 2008
Great Gulf Homes
architectsAlliance
92,810 units/km²

18 YONGE 2006
Lanterra, HR Developments,
Malibu Investments
Page + Steele/IBI Group Architects
115,592 units/km²

JAMES COOPER MANSION 2011
Tridel
Burka Architects, Goldsmith Borgal
129,062 units/km²

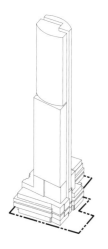

AURA 2015
Canderel
Graziani + Corazza Architects
143,866 units/km²

BURANO CONDOS 2012
Lanterra Developments,
Dov Capital
architectsAlliance
60,593 units/km²

LIBRARY DISTRICT 2014
Context Development
KPMB
140,000 units/km²

LUMIERE CONDOS 2011
Menkes
Wallman Architects
118,387 units / km²

THE YARDS 2013
Onni Group
Wallman Architects
117,444 units / km²

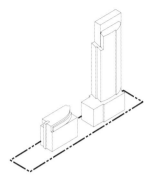

OCEAN CLUB WATERFRONT
2015
Graywood Developments
Page + Steele / IBI Group Architects
94,522 units / km²

TANGO 2014
Concord Adex
Page + Steele / IBI Group Architects
71,283 units / km²

THE FLORIAN 2013
Diamante Development
Hariri Pontarini, Young + Wright
39,708 units / km²

X CONDOS 2010
Great Gulf Homes
architectsAlliance
101,392 units / km²

OBJECTS – POINT TOWER PAIRS

Point tower pairs are large condo developments located on large rectangular sites; they are typically connected by a podium. It is common for the towers to be nearly identical in form and expression, although sometimes one tower will be taller than the other.

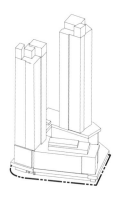

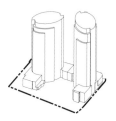

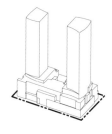

MAPLE LEAF SQUARE 2011
Lanterra, Cadillac Fairview,
Maple Leaf Sports
KPMB, Page + Steele/IBI Group
Architects
95,092 units/km²

MATRIX 2002
Concord Adex
Page + Steele/IBI Group Architects
95,775 units/km²

THE MADISON 2016
Madison Homes
Kirkor Architects + Planners
104,998 units/km²

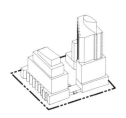

MINTO MIDTOWN 2007
Minto Group
SOM, Ziedler Partnership
Architects
115,967 units/km²

VOYAGER 2005
Monarch Group
Graziani + Corazza Architects
61,484 units/km²

THE MET 2008
Edilcan Development
Page + Steele/IBI Group Architects
92,810 units/km²

U CONDOS 2016
Pemberton Group
architectsAlliance
142,342 units/km^2

CLEAR SPIRIT, GOODERHAM
2012, 2014
Cityscape Development Corp,
Dream
architectsAlliance
123,310 units/km^2

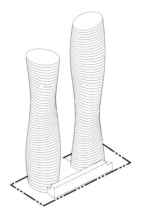

ABSOLUTE WORLD 2011
Fernbrook Home
MAD Architects
114,835 units/km^2

MURANO CONDOS 2010
Lanterra Developments,
Dov Capital
architectsAlliance
204,193 units/km^2

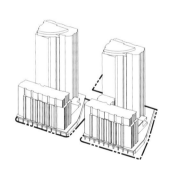

AVONSHIRE 2011
Tridel
Kirkor Architects + Planners
62,430 units/km^2

INFINITY CONDOS 2007, 2008
Conservatory Group
Richmond Architects
43,590 units/km^2

OBJECTS – COMPLEXES

Extra large condo complexes are those with three or more point towers on extra large sites by a single developer. The towers are either constructed concurrently or consecutively, and are frequently connected at grade or in the air through bridges or podiums.

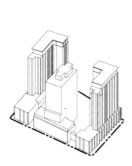

BATTERY PARK CONDOS 2006, 2009, 2011
Monarch Group
Graziani + Corazza Architects
80,206 units / km²

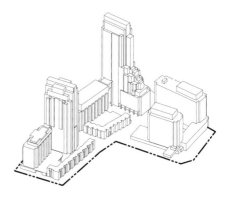

WEST HARBOUR CITY / YORK HARBOUR CLUB
2011, 2014
Plaza
Quadrangle Architects
66,346 units / km²

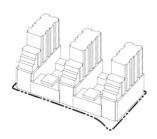

KING WEST CONDOMINIUMS 2013
Plaza, Greybrook Capital
Quadrangle Architects, Gabriel Bodor Architect
151,838 units / km²

PARADE 2011, 2013
Concord Adex
Kohn Pedersen Fox Architects
123,210 units / km²

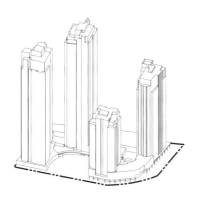

PINACLE CENTRE 2006, 2007, 2011
Pinnacle International
Page + Steele / IBI Group Architects
134,286 units / km²

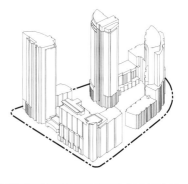

WATERPARK CITY CONDOS 2006, 2007
Lanterra Developments, Lifetime Developments
Page + Steele / IBI Group Architects
121,057 units / km²

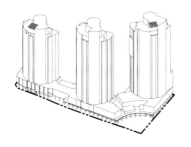

WATERCLUB CONDOMINIUMS 2004, 2005
Kotler Property Corporation
Kirkor Architects + Planners
102,367 units / km²

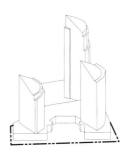

BEYOND THE SEA 2011, 2012
Empire Communities
E.I. Richmond Architects
92,057 units / km²

OBJECTS – INFILL

Shorter infill condo developments (that nevertheless typically feature more than ten floors)
are often located on very narrow or awkwardly shaped sites with neighbours on either side.

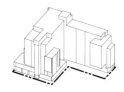

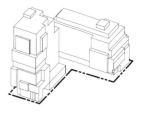

10 MORRISON 2008
Freed Developments
CORE Architects
63,750 units / km²

SEVENTY5 PORTLAND 2010
Freed Developments
CORE Architects & Philippe Starck
70,491 units / km²

SIX50 2012
Freed Deelopments
CORE Architects
76,695 units / km²

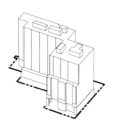

THE KING EAST 2013
Hyde Park Homes,
Lamb Development Corp
CORE Architects
132,226 units / km²

VICTORY CONDOS 2011
Lifetime Developments,
DLVD Developments
Wallman Architects
78,200 units / km²

EAST LOFTS 2010
Lamb Development Corp
architectsAlliance
84,313 units / km²

REVE 2011
Tridel
Wallman Architects &
Burka Architects
96,520 units/km²

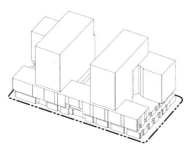

DNA3 2014
Canderel Residential
Graziani & Corazza Architects
83,800 units/km²

B.STREET CONDOS 2014
Lindvest Properties
Hariri Pontarini Architects
62,700 units/km²

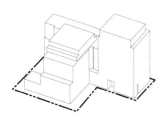

MINTO 775 2013
Minto Group
Hariri Pontarini Architects
79,690 units/km²

MOZO 2004
Context Developments
architectsAlliance
99,763 units/km²

MUSEUM HOUSE ON BLOOR
2013
Yorkville Corporation
Page + Steele/IBI Group Architects
4,918 units/km²

UNITS – ZERO BEDROOMS

Often called studios or bachelor apartments, these unit types are the smallest units available on the market. There is limited, if any, distinction between sleeping, living, and eating quarters. Bathrooms in zero bedroom units are usually the same size as bathrooms in just about every other unit type and are proportionally very large.

3-XXVIII 2015
Five Saint Joseph
399 ft²

TEAL 2012
Limelight Condominiums
450 ft²

347 2016
Picasso Condos
347 ft²

3-XXX 2015
Five Saint Joseph
418 ft²

ALIA 450 2015
CHAZ Yorkville
378 ft²

BT BACHELOR 2014
Edge on Triangle Park
352 ft²

GABRIEL 2015
Bisha
450 ft²

SYDNEY 2015
Bisha
389 ft²

HEATHER 2015
Harmony Village
435 ft²

G24 2017
Dundas Square Gardens
335 ft²

BEDFORD PARK 2018
11 Wellesley
343 ft²

LI 345C 2019
Fortune at Fort York
345 ft²

UNITS – ONE BEDROOM, ONE BAY

This very narrow and long unit type maximizes the number of desirable one-bedroom units. The challenge of this unit type is in meeting building code requirements for bedrooms, which require the latter to have natural light. This is often accomplished with sliding glass doors or interior windows.

1C 2015
Aura on College Park
584 ft²

B3A 2015
King + Condos
580 ft²

W1C4 2014
Edge on Triangle Park
507 ft²

TONY 2016
ME Living Condos
513 ft²

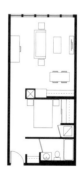

1206 2012
SIX50 King
553 ft²

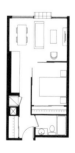

COURT 2018
Yonge & Rich
496 ft²

COLLINS 2017
488 University
544 ft²

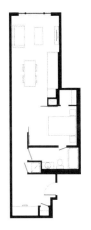

IWI 662 2015
CHAZ Yorkville
662 ft²

PORTLAND 2011
Victory Condos
680 ft²

AQUA 2017
Blue Diamond
500 ft²

1A 2015
Aura on College Park
518 ft²

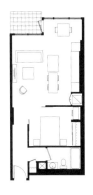

SUITE IV 2015
Five St. Joseph
615 ft²

UNITS – ONE BEDROOM, TWO BAYS

The one-bedroom, two-bay unit type is typically a wider unit in which both the living room and the bedroom have windows to the exterior. The two bays are always divided in the same way, with the kitchen and living room occupying one bay and the bedroom and bathroom occupying the second bay.

RIVA DEL LAGO 2016
555 ft²

700 2014
Emerland Park
655 ft²

SPRUCE 2012
Limelight Condominiums
555 ft²

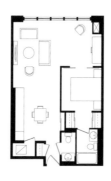

IX 2015
Five Saint Joseph
660 ft²

PEONY 2017
Harmony Village
730 ft²

THE BLOCK 2015
PSV2
531 ft²

491-2 2016
Picasso Condos
491 ft^2

THE LONGMOOR – H 2016
Daniels Erin Mills
621 ft^2

THE PASHA 2012
Miracle in Mississauga
625 ft^2

B5 2015
King + Condos
595 ft^2

THE CHARLES SUITE 2008
18 Yorkville
530 ft^2

THE ATHENS 2008
One Park Towers
641 ft^2

UNITS – ONE BEDROOM PLUS DEN

One-bedroom-plus-den units offer greater flexibility than one-bedroom units; however, this has less to do with square footage and more to do with the arrangement of the bathroom(s). This unit type often offers the possibility of a 'rentable' den by virtue of the placement of the bathroom. If the bathroom is en-suite, it can be accessed from a separate entrance, or it is divorced from the master bedroom altogether. In some cases, the one-bedroom-plus-den may feature a second bathroom with a bath or shower (tellingly, it's never a powder room).

HAYWORTH 2011
Festival Tower
674 ft²

THE ROSEHILL 2011
Chicago Condo
696 ft²

700 2011
Reve Condos
645 ft²

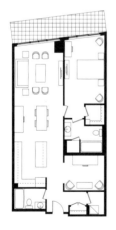

FENTON 2011
Northshore Condos
1030 ft²

BUTTERFLY 2014
Love Condos
620 ft²

ONE BEDROOM + DEN 2015
Exhibit Residences
732 ft²

IX 2015
Five Saint Joseph
660 ft^2

C5 2014
King + Condos
695 ft^2

THE BELMONT A SUITE 2008
18 Yorkville
723 ft^2

MODEL C6 2016
383 Sorauren
696 ft^2

DILLION 2015
Bisha
662 ft^2

DENISON 2018
Yonge + Rich
656 ft^2

UNITS – TWO BEDROOMS, TWO BAYS

The two-bedroom, two-bay unit type is a hybrid of two unit types: the one-bedroom, two-bay and the one-bedroom, one-bay. Second bedrooms without exterior exposure feature interior windows or glass sliding doors.

ROBINSON 2018
Yonge + Rich
766 ft²

WF 2014
2150 Condos
637 ft²

MUSKOKA 2011
Northshore Condos
1,097 ft²

THE CHELSEA 2019
The Britt
750 ft²

307 2012
SIX50 King
1,255 ft²

MAUD 2011
Victory Condos
920 ft²

THE WILLOW 2012
Limelight Condominiums
874 ft²

TWO BEDROOM 2014
Downtown Condos
956 ft²

UNITS – TWO BEDROOMS, THREE BAYS

The two-bedroom, three-bay unit provides equal exposure to all bedrooms, similar to one-bedroom, two-bay units. Here the units shift from long and narrow aspect ratios to more square or wide and shallow proportions. The use of structural shear walls as intra-unit bay dividers are more common in this unit type.

4-L 2011
Absolute World
840 ft²

784 2016
Picasso Condos
784 ft²

2D 2014
Jasmine Condos
769 ft²

CARROLL 2011
Northshore Condos
1,077 ft²

896 2014
Emerald Park
854 ft²

TWO BEDROOM + DEN 2015
Exhibit Residences
1,068 ft²

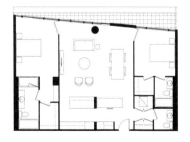

PH-25 2017
Waterlink at Pier 27
1,242 ft²

817 2016
Riva del Lago
817 ft²

UNITS – RESIDUAL

These units result from the logistical complexity of buildings and the economic pressures and time constraints on architects to resolve units into something workable, no matter how inefficient, unusual, or unseemly. Common features of these units include large, ill-defined areas of circulation, columns occupying prime locations, narrow passageways, ineffective room layouts, and poorly located closets and doors.

E1B+D1 2014
Edge on Triangle Park
576 ft²

P-086 2013
Waterlink at Pier 27
675 ft²

PH-47 2012
Waterlink at Pier 27
1384 ft²

LO-K3 2014
L Tower
643 ft²

C688 2016
Totem Condos
688 ft^2

1002 2015
12 Degrees
893 ft^2

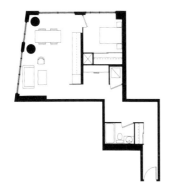

303 2019
Bennet on Bayview
771 ft^2

B503 2016
Totem Condos
503 ft^2

MARKETING – SLOGANS

Rarely do the slogans used to promote and advertise condos make direct references to the building itself. This lack of specificity suggests that any slogan could essentially be applied to any building; however, it is precisely their generic quality that allows prospective buyers to project themselves onto the aspirational lifestyle promises the marketing team is selling.

"Reshaping the Toronto skyline"
AURA 2014

"Wish upon a blue diamond"
BLUE DIAMOND 2017

"Joyful moments.
From a joyful home."
87 PETER 2016

"Condos for contemporary
urban living"
CHAZ YORKVILLE 2015

"[A] modern canvas for personal
design expression"
FASHION HOUSE LOFTS 2014

"Close to everything.
Far from ordinary"
SOUL CONDOS 2017

"Totally awesome.
Totally different."
ENIGMA LOFTS 2016

"Welcome home to the
best of everything"
FESTIVAL TOWER 2011

"Raw. Organic. Unscripted"
TEN93 QUEEN WEST 2016

"If a condominium could be
compared to a film, Festival Tower
would sweep the Oscars"
FESTIVAL TOWER 2011

"Live your life as an exclamation"
**FORWARD CONDOMINIUMS +
NEWTON CONDOMINIUMS** 2017

"If you're not moving forward,
you're moving backward"
**FORWARD CONDOMINIUMS +
NEWTON CONDOMINIUMS** 2017

"The height of originality"
EXHIBIT 2015

"Introducing the epitome of refined
luxury living...superlative features and
finishes and the most radiant views
in Toronto. Experience the brilliance"
BLUE DIAMOND 2017

"You're one of a kind, not one
of the crowd. You make your own
waves and your home is a
refuge of refinement... A more
personal experience; right on
the waterfront"
RIVA DEL LAGO 2017

"The art of change"
ART SHOPPE CONDOS 2019

"With its whimsical and futuristic
design by none other than
globally renowned creative god,
Philippe Stark, Seventy5 Portland
is a Mecca for Toronto-based
design aficionados"
SEVENTY5 PORTLAND 2010

"Own the sky"
PANORAMA AT CITY PLACE 2010

"Downtown Toronto's main event"
DUNDAS SQUARE GARDENS 2017

"Toronto to the core"
88 SCOTT 2017

"Bisha is…
- Attitude: living your life where
  you want it.
- Altitude Piercing
- Presence: Transformation
  of Toronto into a cosmopolitan
  international destination
  with the environment it has
  been missing.
- Style: Seduced by world renowned
  chefs in a boutique environment
  for urban tastemakers.
- Sleek: Complimenting the rarified
  air you already command.
- Birth, Vibrant, International,
  Atmosphere, Freedom, Access,
  Reflecting, Playful, Taste"
  BISHA 2015

"Bisha is social. Embracing your
world behind the velvet ropes, the
hippest edge of culture, entertainment,
fashion and music. Discovering your
new order of experience, imagination,
and independence. Exploring your
boundaries of attitude, awareness,
attention & affection. Sensing with
touch, feel and words with those
of your kind. Bisha will radiate all the
sensory pleasures you desire."
BISHA 2015

"Built for refined living"
BLYTHWOOD AT HUNTINGTON 2015

"Yonge at heart.
Rich in possibilities"
YONGE + RICH 2018

"The city's most connected address"
87 PETER 2017

"Imagine a world without X
Se_
Generation_
_ Rated
ero
_Files
Clima_
_anadu
_ray
_bo_
Se_ In the City
The _ Files
Fo_ _
Lu_ury
Mo_ie
E_tra
E_ude
E_pose
Gala_y"
X CONDOS 2010

"Download the Yonge + Rich
mobile app today. It's like having
a sales centre in your pocket!"
YONGE + RICH 2010

"Bisha will be a fusion of your
life and loves, your naughty and nice,
your dreams and desires"
BISHA 2015

"We understand that first
impressions are lasting"
ME LIVING CONDOS 2016

MARKETING – SUPERNATURAL

Some condo marketing materials depict buildings experiencing or causing supernatural phenomena. These types of visualizations often express idiomatic intentions like "Thinking Outside the Box" or "Breaking New Ground." In some cases these marketing concepts are visually imposed on the architecture itself, whereas in others they are so divorced from the building it becomes hard to understand what exactly the ad is promoting.

LIMELIGHT CONDOMINIUMS 2012
The Daniels Corporation
Kirkor Architects + Planners

FABRIK CONDOS 2015
Menkes Developments
Giannone Petricone Associates

ENIGMA ON THE PARK 2016
Aragon Properties
Quadrangle Architects

DANIELS ERIN MILLS 2016
The Daniels Corporation
Kirkor Architects + Planners

STUDIO ON RICHMOND 2015
Aspen Ridge Homes
Quadrangle Architects Inc.

NEON CONDOS 2016
Pemberton Group, Felcorp
Graziani + Corazza Architects

SCENIC ON EGLINTON 2016
Aspen Ridge Homes
Page + Steele / IBI Group Architects

DANIELS WATERFRONT 2019
The Daniels Corporation
Giannone Petricone Associates Inc.

MARKETING – GHOSTS

"Ghosting" is a strategy used in renderings of buildings on constrained sites. The neighbouring buildings are "ghosted out" to reveal an unhampered view of the proposed building.

VIBE AT BATTERY PARK 2010
Monarch Group
Graziani + Corazza Architects Inc.

EDGE AT TRIANGLE PARK 2013
Urbancorp
TACT Architecture

EXHIBIT RESIDENCES 2016
Bazis Group, Metropia, Plaza
Rosario "Roy" Varacalli

CORE CONDOS 2017
CentreCourt Developments
Page + Steele / IBI Group Architects

E CONDOS 2017
Bazis Group, Metropia, RioCan
Rosario "Roy" Varacalli

COUTURE THE CONDOMINIUM 2013
Monarch Group, Philmor Group
Graziani + Corazza Architects

RIVA DEL LAGO 2016
Mattamy Homes, Biddington Group
Graziani + Corazza Architects

1 YORKVILLE 2018
Bazis Group, Plaza
Rosario "Roy" Varacalli

DIAMOND ON YONGE 2020
Diamante Development
Scott Shields Architects

411 CHURCH STREET 2020
CentreCourt Developments
Page + Steele / IBI Group Architects

MARKETING – BEACONS

To distinguish their buildings from similar-looking projects located in dense urban areas developers will sometimes render their buildings as "beacons" on the skyline. The most recent rendering trend has seen a transition away from glowing edifices to condos set in a crown of spotlights.

COUTURE 2013
Monarch Group and Philmor Group
Graziani + Corazza Architects

AURA AT COLLEGE PARK 2014
Canderel
Graziani + Corazza Architects

1 THOUSAND BAY 2016
Cresford Development Corporation
architectsAlliance

HARBOUR PLAZA RESIDENCES 2017
Menkes Developments Ltd.
architectsAlliance

EAU DU SOLEIL 2018
Empire Communities
Zeidler Partnership Architects

BACKSTAGE 2016
Cityzen Development Group,
Fernbrook Homes
Page + Steele / IBI Group Architects

KEY WEST CONDOS 2016
Times Group Corporation
Burka Architects Inc.

DUNDAS SQUARE GARDENS 2017
Easton's Group of Hotels
Page + Steele / IBI Group Architects

ROSEDALE ON BLOOR CONDOS 2019
Easton's Group of Hotels
Page + Steele / IBI Group Architects

PIER 27 TOWER 2020
Cityzen Development Group and
Fernbrook Homes
architects Alliance

MARKETING – LOBBIES

Lobbies are frequently portrayed as having spatial and social affinities with office or hotel lobbies, complete with glossy surfaces, a 24-hour concierge service staffed by men dressed in suits, grand or moody lighting, and attractive, fashionable condo dwellers dressed for a night out.

SOUTH BEACH CONDOS 2012
Amexon Development Corporation
Arsenault Architects

BACKSTAGE 2016
Cityzen Development Group, Fernbrook Homes
Page + Steele / IBI Group Architects

FABRIK CONDOS 2016
Menkes Developments
Giannone Petricone Associates

BISHA HOTEL & RESIDENCES 2017
Lifetime Developments, Ink Entertainment
Wallman Architects

488 UNIVERSITY 2017
Amexon Development Coporation
CORE Architects

ZIGG CONDOS 2018
Madison Homes, Fieldgate Homes
Kirkor Architects + Planners

MARKETING – LOUNGES

Lounges are commonly featured in new condo buildings and are frequently depicted as bearing resemblances to bars or restaurants, sometimes featuring as many people as one might find in those venues. According to most marketing materials, condo lounges are where beautiful young people sporting the latest fashions flirt, drink, and frolic.

775 KING WEST 2013
Minto
Hariri Pontarini Architects

FASHION HOUSE LOFTS 2014
Freed Developments
CORE Architects

CHAZ YORKVILLE 2015
Edenshaw Homes
Page + Steele / IBI Group Architects

3018 YONGE CONDOS IN LAWRENCE PARK 2016
Lanterra Developments
Hariri Pontarini Architects

TEAHOUSE 2018
Lanterra
architectsAlliance

EAU DU SOLEIL 2018
Empire Communities
Zeidler Partnership Architects

MARKETING – TERRACES

Terraces are the outdoor equivalent of lounges. Although only useable a few months of the year due to Toronto's climate, they figure prominently in promotional materials. Terrace imagery usually features fashionable young people enjoying intimate yet lively social encounters against the backdrop of a night sky.

775 KING WEST 2013
Minto
Hariri Pontarini Architects

AURA AT COLLEGE PARK 2014
Canderel
Graziani + Corazza Architects

CHAZ YORKVILLE 2015
Edenshaw Homes
Page + Steele / IBI Group Architects

3018 YONGE CONDOS IN LAWRENCE PARK 2016
Lanterra Developments
Hariri Pontarini Architects

BISHA HOTEL & RESIDENCES 2017
Lifetime Developments, Ink Entertainment
Wallman Architects

EAU DU SOLEIL 2018
Empire Communities
Zeidler Partnership Architects

MARKETING – POOLS

Marketing materials are often dominated by pools and pool decks invariably featuring attractive, bikini-clad women. Despite their high cost, which translates into higher maintenance fees, pools remain an attractive selling point. Some pools are outdoors and as such can only be used three or four months of the year.

SOUTH BEACH CONDOS 2012
Amexon Development Corporation
Arsenault Architects

ONE BLOOR EAST 2016
Great Gulf Homes
Hariri Pontarini Architects

BACKSTAGE 2016
Cityzen Development Group, Fernbrook Homes
Page + Steele / IBI Group Architects

EAU DU SOLEIL 2018
Empire Communities
Zeidler Partnership Architects

YONGE & RICH 2018
Great Gulf
architectsAlliance

MINTO WESTSIDE 2018
Minto
Wallman Architects

PUBLIC ART

Toronto condos frequently feature a public art component as mandated by city bylaws. Public art is often manifest as either sculptural work or embellished architectural details in the form of coloured lighting accents or custom fences.

RISING 2012
Zhang Huan
Shangri-La Condominiums
Westbank Corporation

ICEBERG BENCHES 2009
Douglas Coupland
Concord City Place

ECHO 2013
Jim Hodges
NXT Condos

BRICK MAN 2010
Inges Idee
Vu Condo

ROSA NAUTICA 2007
Francisco Gazitua
West One Condos

FLOWER POWER 1967/2010
Marc di Suvero
Concord City Place

APPROACHING RED 2013
Maha Mustafa
Concord City Place

THE BOBBERS 2009
Douglas Coupland
Concord City Place

TERRY FOR MIRACLE MILE 2009
Douglas Coupland
Concord City Place

TOM THOMSON'S CANOE 2009
Douglas Coupland
Concord City Place

MITOSIS 2010
Pierre Poussin
Panorama

MONUMENT FOR THE WAR OF 1812 2008
Douglas Coupland
Malibu Harbourfront Condos

YARD STONES 2014
Adad Hannah
The Yards

WAVE SIDE 2011
Daniel Borins &
Jennifer Marman
West Harbour City

FOUNTAINGROVE 2014
Carlo Cesta & Nesto Krüger
Harbour City

FENCE ON THE LOOSE 2012
Vito Acconci
Water Park City Condos

MONOCEROS 2013
FASTWÜRMS
King West Condominiums

GUARDIANS 2013
Olaf Breuning
King West Condominiums

PERPETUAL MOTION 2011
Francisco Gazitua
Liberty Park

THINGS END 2012
James Carl
Festival Tower

BALLAST 2013
Jed Lind
Charlie Condominium

FAIRGROUNDS 2002
Michel Goulet
Icon Condominium

INVERSION 2011
Eldon Garnet
James Cooper Mansion

SHIFT 2008
Carl Tacon
One St. Thomas Residences

DOUBLE TAKE 2014
Shayne Dark
X2 Condos

FOUR SEASONS 2014
Douglas Coupland
Emerald City Condominiums

IMMIGRANT FAMILY 2006
Tom Otterness
18 Yonge Condominiums

STARDUST AND TIME 2011
John McEwen
Luna

BACK TO FRONT 2014
Jason Bruges
300 Front St. West

UNTITLED (FOUNTAIN)
2012
Claude Cormier
Four Seasons

**CANADA'S FIRST POST
OFFICE** 2010
Vu Condos

SKY BRIDGE PATTERNS
2011
Erwin Redl
Battery Park Condos

COLOUR SCHEMES

The following colour swatches were generated by running photographs and renderings of buildings through an algorithm to average out colours and distill them into swatches. The relative length of each palette represents the prevelence of that colour in the colour scheme.

MOZO 2004
Context Developments
architectsAlliance

18 YORKVILLE 2008
Great Gulf Homes
architectsAlliance

CHICAGO CONDO 2010
The Daniels Corporation
Kirkor Architects + Planners

PANORMA 2010
Concord Adex
Page + Steel / IBI, Quandrangle Architects

ABSOLUTE WORLD 2011
Cityzen Development Group,
Fernbrook Homes, MAD, Burka

FESTIVAL TOWER 2011
The Daniels Corporation
KPMB Architects, Kirkor Architects

JAMES COOPER MANSION 2011
Tridel
Burka Architects

NORTH SHORE CONDOS 2011
Slokker Real Estate Group
Giannone Petricone Associates

REVE CONDOS 2011
Tridel
Burka Architects, Wallman Architects

WATERLINK AT PIER 27 2011
Cityzen Development Group, Fernbrook
Homes, architectsAlliance

WIDESUITES CONDOMINIUMS 2011
Conservatory Group
Richmond Architects

LIMELIGHT CONDOMINIUMS 2012
The Daniels Corporation
Kirkor Architects + Planners

PALAIS AT PORT ROYAL PLACE 2012
Pemberton Group
Burka Architects

PARC NUVO AT ESSEX 2012
Tridel
Graziani + Corazza Architects

South Beach Condos 2012
Amexon Development Coporation
Arsenault Architect

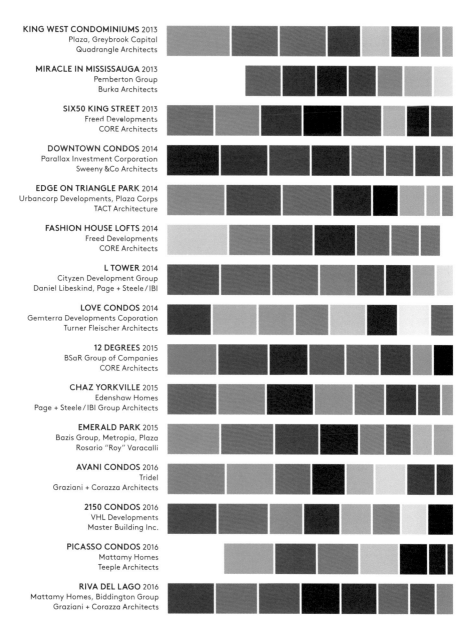

KING WEST CONDOMINIUMS 2013
Plaza, Greybrook Capital
Quadrangle Architects

MIRACLE IN MISSISSAUGA 2013
Pemberton Group
Burka Architects

SIX50 KING STREET 2013
Freed Developments
CORE Architects

DOWNTOWN CONDOS 2014
Parallax Investment Corporation
Sweeny &Co Architects

EDGE ON TRIANGLE PARK 2014
Urbancorp Developments, Plaza Corps
TACT Architecture

FASHION HOUSE LOFTS 2014
Freed Developments
CORE Architects

L TOWER 2014
Cityzen Development Group
Daniel Libeskind, Page + Steele / IBI

LOVE CONDOS 2014
Gemterra Developments Coporation
Turner Fleischer Architects

12 DEGREES 2015
BSaR Group of Companies
CORE Architects

CHAZ YORKVILLE 2015
Edenshaw Homes
Page + Steele / IBI Group Architects

EMERALD PARK 2015
Bazis Group, Metropia, Plaza
Rosario "Roy" Varacalli

AVANI CONDOS 2016
Tridel
Graziani + Corazza Architects

2150 CONDOS 2016
VHL Developments
Master Building Inc.

PICASSO CONDOS 2016
Mattamy Homes
Teeple Architects

RIVA DEL LAGO 2016
Mattamy Homes, Biddington Group
Graziani + Corazza Architects

MANIFESTO

BEAUTY EMERGES WHEN DESIGN MISBEHAVES

PARTISANS

This is the story of Toronto's condo towers, and a call to action for how we can become better city builders.

It's time to call a spade a spade. We haven't been doing our collective best to build a more imaginative, more intelligent, more sustainable, more beautiful city. This isn't about finger-pointing and blame-gaming. Nor is it about lamenting what Toronto is not, i.e., NYC, Paris, London, Barcelona, Chicago, Tokyo, or wringing our hands over whether Toronto is "world class" enough yet.

No, this is about loving Toronto and finding new ways to give it the love it deserves. This is about coming together to renew our commitment to city building. This is about dropping the "play it safe" attitude and seizing the opportunity to do things differently—to reinvent processes and build bolder, more dynamic architecture of all shapes and sizes. This is a plea for diversity, hybridity, invention, and risk-taking. This is a call to action: It's time to revolutionize the process by which architecture gets approved and built in this city and rededicate ourselves to the practice of intelligent, provocative, and beautiful design.

Boom Goes the Condo
Nothing epitomizes Canada's turn-of-the-last-century housing boom more so than the condominium. In a relatively short amount of time, the high-rise condominium has singlehandedly transformed cityscapes right across the country. The sheer ubiquity and relative uniformity of towers—from their glass façades and anemic colour schemes, dominated by grays, greens, and beiges, to their rectangular volumetrics and rigid floor plans—have become the condominium's most distinctive features. Favourable economic forces have created the conditions for the brisk densification of downtown cores. The advent—and virulence—of the condo tower has enabled the vertical urbanization, and arguably, suburbanization, of city centres.

The rise and sprawl of condo towers is an international phenomenon, but in the last decade, it has gripped Toronto more so than almost any other city in the world. Case in point: Between 2008 and 2012, construction was started on approximately 20,000 new condo units per year. These numbers are all the more astonishing precisely because they defy logic.

Even as the U.S. housing market was collapsing and the global economy tumbling in its wake, Toronto was on a residential high-rise construction tear.

Unfortunately, though, we have been giving the city's skyline a piece-meal facelift its citizens have already started to regret. Why have bland condominium designs had so much success in this city? Is it simply the result of successful financial recipes? What are the practical and cultural circumstances contributing to the condominiumization of our city? Despite vacillating real estate predictions, Toronto remains a desirable, growing city, and condos will invariably continue to be built. What needs to change so that the next wave of development is guided by smarter processes and yields better results?

Safety First

Canada's bullish condo sector owes its exponential growth to several factors, including immigration, urbanization, and the two major financial crises that have defined the twenty-first century thus far: the bursting of the tech bubble in 2000, which spurred people to invest in tangible assets, especially property, and the Great Recession. In 2008-09, when the subprime mortgage debacle plunged the U.S. and the rest of the world into near collapse, Canada emerged less scathed due to a more regulated banking system, widely deemed to be one of the safest in the world. Consequently, Canada came to be considered a safe haven for domestic and foreign investment: demand for real estate spiked; the availability of urban land for new building shrunk; housing prices climbed; and condo development soared. Domestic and international investors swooped in to buy up units, driving up prices even more and turning condos into the new de facto rental supply.

One of Canadians' most cherished national narratives is reflected in the international community's impression of our country: that Canada is "safe." Indeed, our reputation for cautious banking policies, a robust real estate market, prioritizing health and education, and offering moderate military support is cause for much pride and admiration. Yet, this logic of safety—of "playing it safe"—also seems to stymy our appetite for inno-vation. Safety has come to define our urban architectural practices, curb-ing our nation's enthusiasm for more intrepid, forward-thinking design.

Safety is another name for risk management, and risk management is a core tenet of real estate development. The urbanization of Toronto has in large part been driven by developers. In order to offset costs in the face of steadily rising property prices, developers need to build quickly—which is to say, economically. From a design perspective, it is hard not to see the ubiquitous condominium tower as a material manifestation of the developer's profit margin—the economic and economical logic used to justify its erection. It doesn't require a tremendous leap of imagination to see that Toronto's skyline has literally come to resemble a series of nondescript columnar extrusions, much like the ones that characterize a Microsoft Excel grid. Effectively, we are building spreadsheets in the sky.

Condominium construction in Toronto more or less corresponds to a version of assembly line architecture in which "design" is viewed as an add-on. Emboldened by a successful yet unimaginative interpretation of the *Tall Building Design Guidelines* that ultimately seeks to expedite construction and maximize return on investment, developers, in conjunction with architects, planners, politicians, and community groups, engage in a rote approval process that all too often arrives at the same, disappointing result: a copy-and-paste architecture driven by expediency and dollar signs. Attempts to jeuje up the exterior with accents, pops of colour, or public art are after-the-fact cosmetic interventions that are often mediocre at best. Instead of using design thinking to guide the process from the outset, design is instead treated like an upgrade, something you can slap on a façade or plop down on the frontage *post hoc*.

The proliferation of insipid towers is essentially the mass production of vertical housing that, with the help of patent brand strategies and faux fancy amenities, masquerades as an aspirational lifestyle choice. Marketing materials target and then attempt to seduce very specific demographics. Ultimately, condos are like any other commodity—mass-produced, financially ratified products that preempt choice and manufacture desire in the same turn. Demand has created bland, a lowest common denominator architecture that promises status in the form of sameness. Whereas a single-family house in the suburbs used to symbolize the culmination of the North American

HEIGHT RIDGES

At a certain point in the planning history of Toronto, a height ridge scheme was agreed upon: the silhouette of the skyline would strive to resemble a tent-like canopy. This canopy is held up by clusters of tall buildings and slopes downward where the architecture shifts to mid- and low-rises. We have all in some sense, then, agreed to a skyline that approximates a circus tent comprised of condominium Riemann sums.

1,815′
CN Tower

978′
CBD

673′
L Tower

768′
South Core

Dream—success, prosperity, and social mobility—condos are the new status symbol, especially for millennials and first-time homebuyers. You know you've arrived when you've bought a variation of the same 700-square-foot box your friend bought in a building a few streets over. Yours has a Shopper's Drug Mart, hers has Rexall, and both of you have reception rooms that will sit empty and sad, waiting for a party that will never come. It's probably no coincidence that the accelerated development of downtown coincided with the depletion of available land for development within the Green Belt. The only place for developers to go was up. Essentially, we have collectively turned the sprawl on its side and catapulted it vertically into the air.

A Broken Process ("It's Just The Way Things Are Done")
Okay, okay, maybe we sound a bit harsh. But are we wrong?
To be clear: No one particular person or group of people is at fault for the substandard high-rise architecture that adorns our city. The burden of responsibility lies with all of us. Developers, architects, city officials, and community groups alike are engaged in a broken process that simply isn't promoting innovative or notable urban design. The approval process is formulaic, bureaucratic, and often adversarial, especially between developers and community groups. Developers almost always propose a finished condominium product that seeks to maximize height and density right out of the gate, before any earnest consultation has occurred with citizens and civic leaders about the site and what the surrounding neighbourhood wants and needs. This top-down, cart-before-the-horse approach is equal parts massing for density and lazy branding, and typically no parts engaged creative visioning with stakeholders. For their part, community groups come to meetings with developers simply ready to say no. They come to the table beset by mistrust, poised to resist density at every turn; however, our NIMBYism is not always protecting or advancing the best interests of our communities. Groups typically obsess over height instead of agitating for better design and construction materials. The even stranger thing is that while all parties seem to lament this defective process, we continue to engage in it ad infinitum. The familiar groove justifies its own internal logic: "It's just the way things are done."

The *Tall Building Design Guidelines* aren't really at fault either. In fact, one could argue that they're rife with good intentions. Designed to safeguard against a relapse into the Corbusian "tower in the park" trend that characterized much of Toronto's post-war development, i.e., slab residential high-rises with large, landscaped setbacks, the *Guidelines* are a common sense approach to building for density in three acts: a base building (podium), a middle, and a top, each part playing a role in achieving the objectives of the Official City Plan. The problem is we're adhering to certain guidelines while completely ignoring others. According to the most recent iteration of the *Guidelines*, "[t]all buildings should reflect design excellence and innovation to acknowledge the important civic role tall buildings play in defining the image and liveability of Toronto." They put considerable emphasis on the need for tall buildings to "make a positive contribution to the public realm"; "embrace design creativity and variation in built form and architectural expression, including variation in tower shape, orientation, and the design of each façade for the purpose of visual interest and sustainability"; and "be innovative, but also appropriate in the choice of materials and construction methods to make a long-term, sustainable, high-value contribution to city building."

All of this begs the obvious questions: How many of the dozens of buildings that have gone up in the last decade push the boundaries of "design excellence and innovation"? How are impervious glass façades and redundant chain anchor tenants helping to frame the public realm and animate communities? Where is the "design creativity and variation in built form" that would not only stimulate our senses, but also support street life and commerce? How can we claim with any pride that the buildings we have approved for construction in the last decade are playing an important civic role "in defining the image and liveability of Toronto"? We're increasingly at risk of fulfilling the Doomsday prophecy Jack Diamond and Barton Myers warned about back in 1978. Building density is critical, but doing so in responsible, diverse, and beautiful ways using sustainable materials needs to be the rule, not the exception. We've produced a condominium monoculture that is putting our civic ecosystem at risk. It's time to bet on the long-term cultural and economic prosperity of design if we're serious about cultivating the future of our city.

THE NEW DOOMSDAY: TORONTO EXTRUDED

EXISTING

+ 10 FLOORS

+ 20 FLOORS

+ 30 FLOORS

+ 40 FLOORS

+ 50 FLOORS

+ 60 FLOORS

+ 70 FLOORS

HOW IT'S DONE IN TORONTO

1.

BUY PROPERTIES AND CONSOLIDATE THE ASSEMBLY
Purchase adjoining properties and go through a legal process to consolidate them into a single assembly.

2.

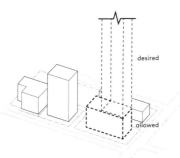

desired

allowed

SITE ACCESS, CORE, AND CIRCULATION
Loading, parking access, and cores are the most demanding and inflexible spatial compo-nents of the ground floor, not to mention the least profitable. As such, they must be figured out first and occupy as little space as possible.

3.

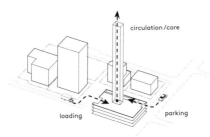

circulation /core

loading

parking

FOLLOW THE DESIGN GUIDELINES FOR PODIUM AND SETBACKS
The building's massing is highly influenced by setbacks, zoning envelopes, and minimum distance requirements from adjacent buildings.

4.

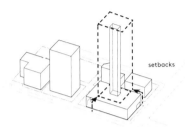

setbacks

REZONE

The allowable building height and FAR are likely to be insufficient for developers' purposes, so one usually applies to have the site rezoned for higher density. This is typically done after the architect has designed the building. Should the rezoning request fail the decision can be appealed by petitioning the Ontario Municipal Board (OMB), which bases its decisions on building precedents in the neighbourhood.

5.

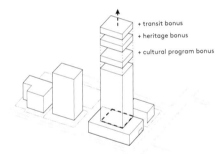

+ transit bonus
+ heritage bonus
+ cultural program bonus

NEGOTIATE AND EXTRUDE

Alternatively, developers can choose to negotiate with the City, offering community benefits in exchange for additional height or floor area.

6.

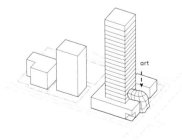

art

ADD PUBLIC ART

Fulfill the negotiated promise by commissioning a public art project for the base of the tower.

PARTISANSHIP

What follows is a statement of our beliefs, ideals, and guiding principles. This framework is the basis upon which we propose a vision for building a better Toronto.

We believe in making the impossible probable. This isn't because we're arrogant wunderkinds who think we can do everything better. It's because we're dreamers and urban activists fuelled by earnest convictions, unbridled enthusiasm, a will to upend the status quo, and a willingness to examine blind spots.

We believe beauty emerges when design misbehaves. Misbehaviour isn't about acting irresponsibly brash. It's about enlisting processes that hack and overturn the status quo. It's the unexpected outcome of enlisting two methodologies: resistance and play. Resistance entails challenging orthodoxy and mediocrity, and embracing challenges to push our design thinking to extremes to generate unconventional solutions. Play is about defusing rote procedures, inventing new tools, tapping the unanticipated, and having fun. We understand misbehaviour as the spark born of resistance and play, the slight mutation or counternarrative that unleashes beauty and reinvents the norm. Resistance, Play, Misbehaviour—RPM—is the high-octane energy that fuels our resolve to go the extra distance.

We believe in the promise of design. Design continues to be orphaned in ways that thwart our nation's potential to thrive, hampering us from setting new precedents as a global leader in urban innovation. Both architecture and design continue to fall through the cracks of government support and policy and infrastructure agendas. At the time of this book's publication, Ontario's Culture Strategy still failed to adequately acknowledge architecture and design as drivers of culture, let alone cultural agents themselves. Moreover, government funding bodies, like the Natural Sciences and Engineering Research Council of Canada (NSERC), lack mechanisms for including and adjudicating architecture's critical contributions to research and development. Design isn't a superfluous luxury; it's the great mediator of siloed disciplines and interests. Put simply, it drives the evolution of civilization. Architects need to do more than just build buildings; they need to advocate for design as a cause itself.

We believe in the power of design thinking. Architecture has increasingly become a form of merchandise that occupies one of two extremes: either a generic, mass-produced, copy-and-paste product, or a fetishized luxury commodity propelled by a generation of Instagrammers who feed on glossy, aspirational images. For architecture to be effective and transporting, the process must be a rigorous, iterative, and playful one that defies conventions and subverts norms. The process itself must misbehave in order to disrupt typological expectations and generate hybrid, beautiful structures that outperform and overdeliver. We need to prioritize vision, context, and human experience. Before we put pen to paper, architects should not only study a site, but also investigate communities in deep, qualitative ways. We need to embed ourselves in neighbourhoods and talk to citizens, business owners, and civic leaders to ascertain their wants and needs. We need to work directly with developers to distill creative visions before design and massing even begin. Let's embrace a bottom-up, community-oriented process that bridges all stakeholders.

We believe in Toronto. Toronto continues to earn top marks on prestigious liveability scorecards and is increasingly garnering the attention of international tastemakers and cultural enthusiasts. We are a powerful, ethnically diverse city that boasts a thriving arts and culture scene. There is so much beauty and variety here, and yet our built environment remains largely banal and monocultural. Design has been left off the menu of our cultural renaissance. If we want Toronto to grow gracefully out of its awkward adolescence, we need to see this banality as a condition of possibility, a blank canvas upon which we can project an architecture that not only distinguishes the city, but also reflects the amazing metropolis we are becoming.

1.   Revolutionize the planning and approval process. Recognize the difference between projects that are merely profit grabs and those that are trying to do something different and reward them. Empower planning. Get rid of the Ontario Municipal Board.

2.   Embrace density. If we resist it, we'll become a city for the 1%, a club for rich people who will be the only ones who can afford to live in Toronto. Under no circumstances can we become that city.

3.   Mix private and public housing. Put public housing in condos.

4.   Put an end to energy-leaking condo balconies. It's time to eliminate everything environmentally unsustainable.

5.   Mutate the buildings. Blur shapes and boundaries to generate innovative hybrid typologies.

6.   Play with podiums. Make them diverse architectural playgrounds that break the city's hermeticism.

7.   Prove that business and beauty make good bedfellows. There's absolutely no reason beautiful design cannot be profitable.

8.   Stop being slaves to software. Invent your own tools. Adopt new technologies, rewrite the code, and collaborate in unexpected ways.

9.   Legislate open juried design competitions for all new projects over thirty stories.

10.   Stop conceiving of public art as an add-on sculpture or accessory. Architecture is art.

11.   Build for 100 years from now.

CREATE HYBRIDITY

Building use has always driven the development of architectural types. Today, the parameters of use and sustainability have expanded. The 21st-century technologies at our disposal make it possible to create hybrid, mutant architectures to support changing needs and accommodate diverse programming.

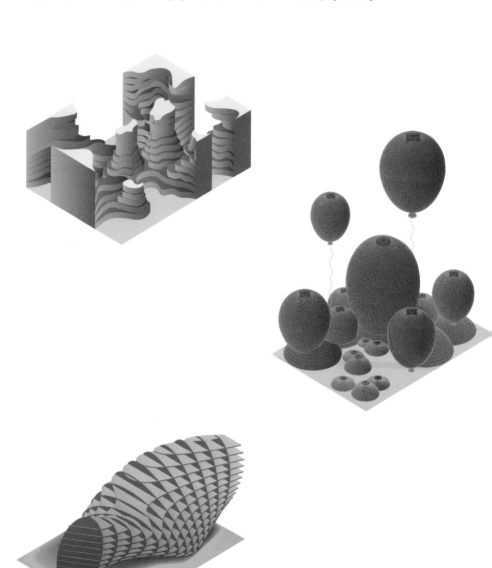

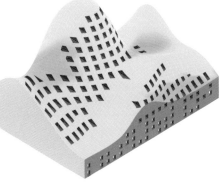

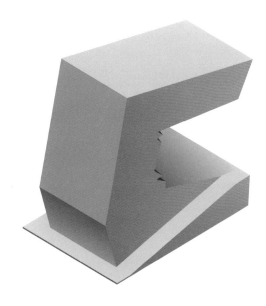

PLAY WITH THE PODIUM

The podium is an opportunity for a condominium project to differentiate itself with respect to civic placemaking at grade. Given their density and importance to the public realm, podiums can be architectural playgrounds that break open the streetscape and drive the economy of the building and the neighbourhood.

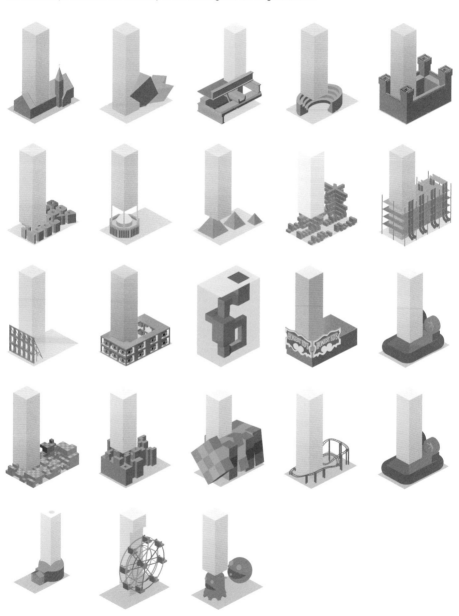

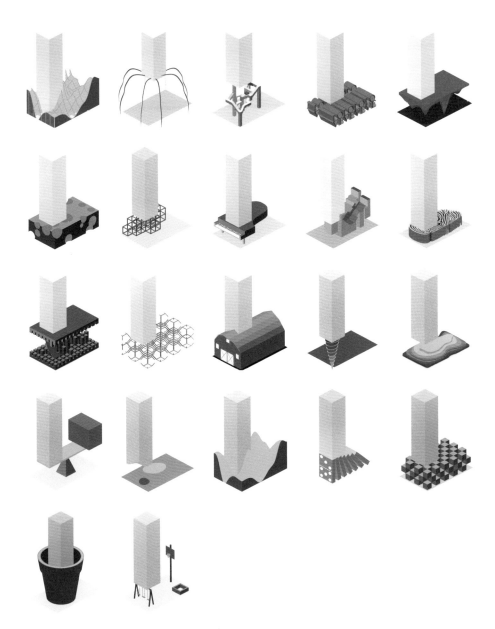

CREDITS

Concept
Hans Ibelings and Alexander Josephson (PARTISANS)

Editor
Nicola Spunt (PARTISANS)

Research and Catalogue
Nathan Bishop (PARTISANS)

Graphic Design
Haller Brun, Amsterdam

Printing
robstolk® Amsterdam

Published by
The Architecture Observer, Montreal/Amsterdam

It was not possible to find all copyright holders of the illustrations used. Interested parties are requested to contact the publisher.

www.architectureobserver.eu
www.partisanprojects.com

ISBN/EAN
978-94-92058-04-1

Images
Jonathan Friedman (PARTISANS): pp. 12–13, 16–17, 22–23, 26–27, 32–33, 36–37, 42–43; NormLi Architectural Graphics and Illustrations: pp. 114–115

With a special thanks to all PARTISANS, and PARTISANS at large:
Pooya Baktash, Betty Vuong, Ivan Vasyliv, Michael Bootsma, Jonathan Friedman, Ariel Cooke, Nour Nasser Agha, Valerie Vicente, Adam Zabunyan, Adriana Mogosanu, Shamir Panchal, Andrew Azzopardi, Robert Jan Van Pelt, Norm Li.